100

pancakes &
waffles
from 1 easy recipe

100

pancakes &
waffles
from 1 easy recipe

First published in 2012
LOVE FOOD is an imprint of Parragon Books Ltd

Parragon
Queen Street House
4 Queen Street
Bath BA1 1HE, UK

ISBN: 978-1-4454-9537-8

Printed in China

Cover design by Talking Design
Written by Christine France
Photography by Clive Bozzard-Hill
Home economy by Valarie Barrett

Notes for the Reader
This book uses imperial, metric, and US cup measurements. Follow
the same units of measurement throughout; do not mix metric and
imperial. All spoon measurements are level: teaspoons are assumed
to be 5 ml, and tablespoons are assumed to be 15 ml. Unless
otherwise stated, milk is assumed to be whole, eggs are large,
individual vegetables are medium, and pepper is freshly ground
black pepper.

The times given are an approximate guide only. Preparation times
differ according to the techniques used by different people and the
cooking times may also vary from those given. Optional ingredients,
variations, or serving suggestions have not been included in the
calculations.

Recipes using raw or very lightly cooked eggs should be avoided
by infants, the elderly, pregnant women, convalescents, and anyone
with a chronic illness. Pregnant and breast-feeding women are
advised to avoid eating peanuts and peanut products. People with
nut allergies should be aware that some of the prepared ingredients
used in the recipes in this book may contain nuts. Always check the
packaging before use.

Contents

Introduction

Who can resist a pile of fresh waffles or pancakes, oozing with maple syrup or with a tasty topping? Many cultures all over the world celebrate this wonderful dish, with many variations. This book is packed with ideas for waffles, pancakes, and crepes, both sweet and savory, for any time of day and every occasion, so you can start cooking right now.

The beauty of this book is that every single recipe is based on the Basic Batter Mix (see page 10). To make life easier for you, we have done the hard work so that each recipe is complete and you won't need to refer back to the basic recipe every time.

Equipment

The equipment needed to make the basic batter is all standard—a mixing bowl, sifter, measuring cups and spoons, and electric mixer. If you're making pancakes or crepes, you'll need a large, solid-bottom griddle pan or skillet and a palette knife or spatula, and for making waffles, you'll need a good-quality waffle iron.

Most waffle irons are electric nowadays, but all cook the batter between two heated, embossed metal plates, making a crisp, golden surface with decorative indentations for holding syrup and other toppings. Most waffle irons make thick, Belgian-style waffles, but some are designed to make thinner, more waferlike waffles. You can choose one that makes square or circular, or even heart-shaped waffles, and some are marked to make easy divisions in the waffles. Look for one that is easy to clean and has adjustable settings, with clear indicator lights or a timer.

Basic Ingredients

The ingredients for a basic batter are all-purpose flour, baking powder, salt, eggs, milk or other liquid, and oil or butter. Baking powder is omitted when making crêpes.

All-purpose white flour can be replaced either partly or entirely with other flours, such as whole wheat, rye or buckwheat flour, cornmeal, or chickpea flour, all giving a different texture and flavor to the finished waffles or pancakes. Cornstarch improves crispness, and gluten-free flours, such as rice or potato flour, provide a softer, heavier result.

The flour is sifted with baking powder to give a risen, spongy texture to waffles and pancakes, and occasionally it's necessary to add a little baking soda to balance the acidity of the mix, such as when using buttermilk or yogurt.

For a sweet batter, sugar is usually added, and this may be any type, depending on the flavor or texture required. Confectioners' sugar and superfine sugar dissolve easily and give a light flavor (to make superfine sugar, process granulated sugar in a food processor or blender for 1 minute), whereas brown sugar adds an extra richness of flavor. Honey and maple syrup are more usually used in toppings, but they can also be added to the batter mix as a sweetener.

Eggs help to give structure to the mix and these may be used whole, or separated, so that the whites can be whisked to give an extra light texture. Extra egg yolks may be added to enrich the batter.

Milk is used as the liquid for most batters and this can be whole, lowfat or skim, or you can use other milks, such as coconut, almond, or soy milk. Buttermilk, cream, or yogurt make a slightly thicker, softer batter with a rich flavor. Fruit juice is used for flavor and to make a light, low-fat batter, and the bubbles in beer help to add lightness. For crepes, where a thinner batter is required, water is usually added to the mix to make more delicate crepes.

Salt is added to batters both savory and sweet, because it helps to strengthen the gluten in the flour, for a light, risen texture.

Flavorings, such as vanilla extract or almond extract, may be added to the basic batter for a subtle flavor, and these can be replaced with other extracts and essences.

Additional Ingredients

Batters are surprisingly versatile, and once you've mastered the basic mix, you can start experimenting with your own favorite flavors.

Finely chopped, grated, or pureed fruits and vegetables not only add flavor to batters, but also boost the nutritional content. Beet or spinach will add an appetizing splash of healthy color to savory waffles and pancakes. Finely chopped fresh herbs are also great for flavor and add a delicate touch of green to all kinds of batters. Pureed or berry fruits can simply be stirred in for natural sweetness.

Whole grains, nuts, and seeds give a crunchy or chewy texture to waffles and pancakes, as well as extra fiber and nutrients.

Spices, both sweet and savory, are an easy addition to all kinds of batters and can really add a special depth of flavor. Sift the spices with the dry ingredients to ensure even distribution.

A splash of strong coffee makes a good flavoring for many sweet batters, and the flavor combines well with nuts and cream or maple syrup toppings.

Chocoholics can add grated chocolate or chocolate chips to thick batters for waffles and pancakes. Cocoa is used for crepe batters.

Top Tips

* Waffle and pancake batters benefit from 5 minutes standing time to allow the leavening agent to activate.

* Let crepe batters stand for 15 minutes minimum, so the starch grains absorb the moisture.

* Thoroughly preheat the waffle iron or skillet before starting to cook.

* Even waffle makers and skillets with a nonstick surface need greasing, so always brush or spray with oil or butter before cooking each batch.

* When cooking waffles, have a preheated oven and hot baking sheet ready to keep them hot and crisp.

* Use a ladle or pitcher to pour the correct amount of batter into the waffle maker or skillet, so it's the same each time.

* Don't overfill the waffle compartments; make sure there is room for the batter to expand.

* Avoid stacking waffles until you're ready to serve to prevent them from turning soft.

* Interleave crepes with paper towels to absorb steam while cooking the remaining batter.

* To freeze waffles or pancakes, cool on a wire rack, pack into plastic bags, seal, and freeze for up to 3 months.

* To freeze crepes, cool quickly, interleave with nonstick parchment paper, place in a plastic bag, seal, and freeze for up to 3 months.

Basic Batter Mix

Makes about 2 cups of batter, enough to make about
8 large waffles, 12 pancakes, or 8 crepes.

* 1¼ cups all-purpose white flour,
  (recipes may substitute whole wheat, buckwheat,
  rye, or rice flours, or fine cornmeal)
* 1½ tsp baking powder (omit from crepes recipes)
* pinch of salt
* 1 cup milk
  (recipes may substitute nondairy milk, such as
  soy or coconut, or buttermilk, yogurt, cream,
  fruit juice, or beer)
* 1 extra-large egg
* 2 tbsp oil or melted butter

This is the basic recipe on which all 100 variations of
waffles, pancakes, and crepes in the book are based.

For each recipe, the basic mix is highlighted (*) for
easy reference, so all you have to do is follow the easy
steps each time and you'll never run out of ideas for
unusual pancakes, waffles, and crepes.

Please note that the basic ingredients may vary from
time to time, so please check these carefully.

Brunch

Blueberry Pancakes with Whipped Butter

1. For the whipped butter, place the butter in a bowl and beat with an electric mixer until softened. Add the milk and maple syrup and beat hard until pale and fluffy.

2. Sift the flour, baking powder, salt, and sugar into a bowl. Add the milk, egg, and oil and beat to a smooth batter. Stir in the blueberries and let stand for 5 minutes.

3. Lightly grease a griddle pan or skillet and heat over medium heat. Spoon tablespoons of batter into the pan and cook until bubbles appear on the surface. Turn over with a spatula or palette knife and cook the other side until golden brown. Repeat this process, using the remaining batter, while keeping the cooked pancakes warm.

4. Serve the pancakes in stacks with extra blueberries, a spoonful of whipped butter, and a drizzle of maple syrup.

Serves 4

- 1¼ cups all-purpose white flour
- 1½ tsp baking powder
- pinch of salt
- 2 tbsp superfine sugar
- 1 cup milk
- 1 extra-large egg
- 2 tbsp sunflower oil, plus extra for greasing
- 1 cup blueberries, plus extra to decorate

Whipped butter
- ½ cup unsalted butter, at room temperature
- 2 tbsp milk
- 1 tbsp maple syrup, plus extra to serve

Buttermilk Pancakes with Mixed Berry Compote

1. For the compote, place the berries, sugar, and lemon juice in a saucepan and heat gently until the sugar dissolves. Stir lightly and keep warm.

2. Sift the flour, baking powder, salt, and sugar into a bowl. Add the buttermilk, egg, and butter and beat to a smooth batter. Let stand for 5 minutes.

3. Lightly grease a griddle pan or skillet and heat over medium heat. Spoon tablespoons of batter into the pan and cook until bubbles appear on the surface. Turn over with a spatula or palette knife and cook the other side until golden brown. Repeat this process, using the remaining batter, while keeping the cooked pancakes warm.

4. Serve immediately with the compote.

Serves 4

- 1¼ cups all-purpose white flour
- 1½ tsp baking powder
- pinch of salt
- 1 tbsp superfine sugar
- 1 cup buttermilk
- 1 extra-large egg
- 2 tbsp melted butter
- sunflower oil, for greasing

Compote
- generous 1 cup raspberries
- 1¼ cups red currants
- 1 cup blackberries
- 3 tbsp superfine sugar
- 1 tbsp lemon juice

Silver Dollar Pancakes with Maple Syrup

1. Sift the flour, baking powder, and salt into a bowl. Add the buttermilk, egg, and butter and beat to a smooth batter. Let stand for 5 minutes.

2. Lightly grease a griddle pan or skillet and heat over medium heat. Spoon small spoonfuls of batter into the pan to make pancakes approximately 1½ inches/4 cm across and cook until bubbles appear on the surface.

3. Turn over with a spatula or palette knife and cook the other side until golden brown. Repeat this process, using the remaining batter, while keeping the cooked pancakes warm.

4. Serve the pancakes in tall stacks, drizzled with maple syrup.

Serves 4–6

* 1¼ cups all-purpose white flour
* 1½ tsp baking powder
* pinch of salt
* 1 cup buttermilk
* 1 extra-large egg
* 2 tbsp melted butter
  sunflower oil, for greasing
  maple syrup, to serve

4

Apple & Cinnamon Crepes

1. Sift the flour, cinnamon, and salt into a bowl. Add the milk, apple juice, egg, and butter and beat to a smooth, bubbly batter. Let stand for 15 minutes.

2. For the filling, place the apples, lemon juice, and sugar in a medium saucepan over medium heat, cover, and heat, stirring occasionally, until tender. Keep warm.

3. Put ½ teaspoon of the butter in an 8-inch/20-cm skillet over medium heat. Pour in enough batter to just cover the skillet, swirling to cover in a thin, even layer. Cook until the underside is golden, then flip or turn with a spatula or palette knife and cook the other side until golden brown.

4. Repeat this process, using the remaining batter. Interleave the cooked crepes with paper towels and keep warm.

5. Spoon the apples onto the crepes and fold over into fan shapes. Dust with cinnamon and serve immediately.

Serves 4

* 1¼ cups all-purpose white flour
  1 tsp ground cinnamon, plus extra for dusting
* pinch of salt
* 1 cup milk
  scant ½ cup apple juice
* 1 extra-large egg
* 2 tbsp melted butter
  butter, for frying

Filling
3 apples, peeled and sliced
juice of ½ lemon
2 tbsp superfine sugar

Muesli Pancake Stack with Honey

1. Sift the flour, baking powder, and salt into a bowl. Add the milk, egg, oil, and yogurt and beat to a smooth batter. Stir in the muesli, and let stand for 5 minutes.

2. Lightly grease a griddle pan or skillet and heat over medium heat. Spoon tablespoons of batter into the pan and cook until bubbles appear on the surface.

3. Turn over with a spatula or palette knife and cook the other side until golden brown. Repeat this process, using the remaining batter, while keeping the cooked pancakes warm.

4. Spoon honey over the pancakes and serve immediately.

Serves 4

* 1¼ cups all-purpose white flour
* 1½ tsp baking powder
* pinch of salt
* 1 cup milk
* 1 extra-large egg
* 2 tbsp sunflower oil, plus extra for greasing
  2 tbsp plain low-fat yogurt
  1¼ cups muesli
  honey, to serve

Espresso Waffles with Vanilla Cream

1. For the vanilla cream, place the cream, sugar, and vanilla extract in a bowl and beat until thick enough to just hold its shape.

2. Sift the flour, baking powder, and salt into a bowl. Add the milk, coffee, egg, butter, and sugar and beat to a smooth batter. Let stand for 5 minutes.

3. Lightly grease a waffle maker and heat until hot. Pour the batter into the waffle maker and cook until golden brown. Repeat, using the remaining batter, while keeping the cooked waffles warm.

4. Serve the waffles immediately, topped with a spoonful of cream and dusted with unsweetened cocoa.

Serves 4

* 1¼ cups all-purpose white flour
* 1½ tsp baking powder
* pinch of salt
  ½ cup milk
  ½ cup espresso coffee or strong coffee
* 1 extra-large egg
* 2 tbsp melted butter
  1 tbsp dark brown sugar
  sunflower oil, for greasing
  unsweetened cocoa, for dusting

Vanilla cream
scant 1 cup heavy cream
1 tbsp superfine sugar
1 tsp vanilla extract

Banana Pancakes with Whipped Maple Butter

1. Sift the flour, baking powder, sugar, and salt into a bowl. Add the buttermilk, egg, and butter and beat to a smooth batter. Mash 2 bananas and mix thoroughly into the batter with the orange rind. Let stand for 5 minutes.

2. Lightly grease a griddle pan or skillet and heat over medium heat. Spoon tablespoons of batter into the pan and cook until bubbles appear on the surface.

3. Turn over with a spatula or palette knife and cook the other side until golden brown. Repeat this process, using the remaining batter, while keeping the cooked pancakes warm.

4. For the maple butter, beat the butter and maple syrup together, whisking until light and fluffy.

5. Slice the remaining banana and serve with the pancakes, with the maple butter spooned over.

Serves 4

- 1¼ cups all-purpose white flour
- 1½ tsp baking powder
- 1 tbsp superfine sugar
- pinch of salt
- 1 cup buttermilk
- 1 extra-large egg
- 2 tbsp melted butter
- 3 ripe bananas
- finely grated rind of 1 small orange
- sunflower oil, for greasing

Maple butter
- 6 tbsp butter
- 4 tbsp maple syrup

French Toast Waffles

1. Sift the flour, baking powder, salt, cinnamon, and sugar into a bowl. Add the milk, egg, and butter and beat to a smooth batter. Let stand for 5 minutes.

2. Lightly grease a waffle maker and heat until hot. Dip the slices of bread quickly into the batter, then place in the waffle maker and cook until golden brown. Repeat, using the remaining batter, while keeping the cooked waffles warm.

3. Serve immediately, with melted butter and sugar.

Serves 4

* 1¼ cups all-purpose white flour
* 1½ tsp baking powder
* pinch of salt
  1 tsp ground cinnamon
  2 tbsp superfine sugar
* 1 cup milk
* 1 extra-large egg
* 2 tbsp melted butter, plus extra to serve
  sunflower oil, for greasing
  8–10 slices brioche-type bread
  raw brown sugar, to serve

German Pancakes

1. Preheat the oven to 425°F/220°C. Lightly grease 12 deep cups in a muffin pan and heat in the preheated oven for 5 minutes.

2. Sift the flour and salt into a bowl. Add the milk, eggs, oil, honey, lemon rind, and vanilla extract and beat to a smooth, bubbly batter.

3. Pour the batter into the hot cups, then return the muffin pan to the oven and cook for 20–25 minutes, until the pancakes are well risen and golden brown.

4. Turn out, dust with confectioners' sugar, and serve immediately.

Serves 4–6

- 1¼ cups all-purpose white flour
- pinch of salt
- 1 cup milk
- 2 extra-large eggs
- 2 tbsp sunflower oil, plus extra for greasing
- 2 tbsp honey
- finely grated rind of 1 lemon
- 1 tsp vanilla extract
- confectioners' sugar, for dusting

Tropical Fruit Crepes

1. Sift the flour and salt into a bowl. Add the milk, pineapple juice, egg, butter, and lime zest and beat to a smooth, bubbly batter. Let stand for 15 minutes.

2. For the filling, combine the kiwi, papaya, pineapple, passion fruit, and lime juice in a bowl.

3. Put ½ teaspoon of the butter into an 8-inch/20-cm skillet over medium heat. Pour in enough batter to just cover the skillet, swirling to cover in a thin, even layer. Cook until the underside is golden, then flip or turn with a spatula or palette knife and cook the other side until golden brown.

4. Repeat this process, using the remaining batter. Interleave the cooked crepes with paper towels and keep warm.

5. Place a spoonful of the fruit in the center of each crepe, fold opposite sides over toward the center, decorate with lime zest, and serve immediately.

Serves 4

* 1¼ cups all-purpose white flour
* pinch of salt
* 1 cup milk
  scant ½ cup pineapple juice
* 1 extra-large egg
* 2 tbsp melted butter
  finely grated rind of ½ lime
  butter, for frying
  strips of lime zest, to decorate

Filling
1 kiwi, sliced
1 small papaya, sliced
½ fresh pineapple, sliced
1 passion fruit, halved and scooped out
juice of ½ lime

Pancake Eggs Benedict

1. Sift the flour, baking powder, and salt into a bowl. Add the milk, egg, and butter and beat to a smooth batter. Let stand for 5 minutes.

2. Lightly grease a griddle pan or skillet and heat over medium heat. Spoon tablespoons of batter into the pan and cook until bubbles appear on the surface.

3. Turn over with a spatula or palette knife and cook the other side until golden brown. Repeat this process, using the remaining batter, while keeping the cooked pancakes warm.

4. For the topping, bring a wide saucepan of water to a boil, then reduce the heat to a low simmer. Carefully break the eggs into the water and poach for about 3 minutes, until the whites are set but the yolks are still runny.

5. Meanwhile, place the egg yolks, mustard, and lemon juice in a blender and blend for a few seconds, until smooth. Place the butter in a saucepan and heat until bubbling. With the motor running, gradually pour the butter into the egg yolks until the sauce is thickened and creamy. Season to taste with salt and pepper.

6. Serve immediately, in groups of three overlapping pancakes, with the eggs on top and the sauce spooned over and seasoned with extra pepper.

Serves 4

- 1¼ cups all-purpose white flour
- 1½ tsp baking powder
- pinch of salt
- 1 cup milk
- 1 extra-large egg
- 2 tbsp melted butter
  sunflower oil, for greasing

Topping
4 extra-large eggs
3 egg yolks
½ tsp English mustard
1 tbsp lemon juice
scant 1 cup butter
salt and pepper

Chive Waffles with Scrambled Eggs

1. Sift the flour, baking powder, and salt into a bowl. Add the milk, egg, butter, and chives and beat to a smooth batter. Let stand for 5 minutes.

2. Lightly grease a waffle maker and heat until hot. Pour the batter into the waffle maker and cook until golden brown. Repeat, using the remaining batter, while keeping the cooked waffles warm.

3. For the topping, beat the eggs with the cream and season to taste with salt and pepper. Melt the butter in a medium saucepan over medium heat and add the egg mixture. Stir over low heat until the eggs are lightly set but still creamy.

4. Serve immediately, topped with scrambled eggs, garnished with chives, and seasoned with extra pepper.

Serves 4

* 1¼ cups all-purpose white flour
* 1½ tsp baking powder
* pinch of salt
* 1 cup milk
* 1 extra-large egg
* 2 tbsp melted butter
  4 tbsp finely chopped chives
  sunflower oil, for greasing

Topping
8 eggs
4 tbsp light cream or milk
2 tbsp butter
salt and pepper
chives, to garnish

Blinis with Smoked Salmon

1. Sift the flour, baking powder, and salt into a bowl. Add the milk, egg yolk, butter, and yogurt and beat to a smooth batter. In a separate bowl, whisk the egg whites to soft peaks and fold lightly and evenly into the batter.

2. Lightly grease a griddle pan or skillet and heat over medium heat. Spoon small spoonfuls of batter into the pan and cook until bubbles appear on the surface.

3. Turn over with a spatula or palette knife and cook the other side until golden brown. Repeat this process, using the remaining batter to make 30–36 blinis, while keeping the cooked blinis warm.

4. Place a spoonful of crème fraîche on each blini, top with smoked salmon and a sprig of dill, and serve warm or cold.

Serves 4

- 1¼ cups buckwheat flour
- 1½ tsp baking powder
- pinch of salt
- 1 cup milk
- 1 extra-large egg, separated
- 2 tbsp melted butter
- 3 tbsp plain yogurt
- 1 egg white
- sunflower oil, for greasing

To serve
- ⅔ cup crème fraîche or sour cream
- 12 oz/350 g smoked salmon
- fresh dill sprigs, to garnish

14

Bacon Waffles with Maple Syrup

1. Sift the flour, baking powder, and salt into a bowl. Add the milk, egg and butter, and beat to a smooth batter. Let stand for 5 minutes.

2. Lightly grease a waffle maker and heat until hot. Pour the batter into the waffle maker and cook until golden brown. Repeat, using the remaining batter, while keeping the cooked waffles warm.

3. Meanwhile, preheat a broiler to high, place the bacon on a broiler pan, and broil until crisp and golden brown, turning once.

4. Serve the waffles immediately, topped with bacon and drizzled with maple syrup.

Serves 4

* 1¼ cups all-purpose white flour
* 1½ tsp baking powder
* pinch of salt
* 1 cup milk
* 1 extra-large egg
* 2 tbsp melted butter
  sunflower oil, for greasing
  12 slices bacon
  maple syrup, to serve

Pastrami on Rye Pancakes

1. Sift the flour, baking powder, and salt into a bowl. Add the milk, egg, butter, and yogurt and beat to a smooth batter. Let stand for 5 minutes.

2. Lightly grease a griddle pan or skillet and heat over medium heat. Spoon tablespoonfuls of batter into the pan and cook until bubbles appear on the surface.

3. Turn over with a spatula or palette knife and cook the other side until golden brown. Repeat this process, using the remaining batter, while keeping the cooked pancakes warm.

4. Spread a little mayonnaise on each pancake, top with sliced pastrami and pickle slices, and serve immediately.

Serves 4

1½ cups rye flour
1½ tsp baking powder
pinch of salt
generous 1 cup milk
1 extra-large egg
2 tbsp melted butter
3 tbsp plain yogurt
sunflower oil, for greasing

To serve
4 tbsp mayonnaise
7 oz/200 g sliced pastrami
sliced pickles

Shrimp & Avocado Crepes

1. Sift the flour and salt into a bowl. Add the milk, water, egg, butter, and dill and beat to a smooth, bubbly batter. Let stand for 15 minutes.

2. For the filling, halve, pit, and peel the avocados and slice crosswise. Sprinkle with lemon juice. Combine the shrimp and avocado and season to taste with salt and pepper.

3. Lightly grease an 8-inch/20-cm skillet and heat over medium heat. Pour in enough batter to just cover the skillet, swirling to cover in a thin, even layer. Cook until the underside is golden, then flip or turn with a spatula or palette knife and cook the other side until golden brown.

4. Repeat this process, using the remaining batter. Interleave the cooked crepes with paper towels and keep warm.

5. Divide the filling among the crepes and roll up loosely. Serve immediately with lemon wedges.

Serves 4

* 1¼ cups all-purpose white flour
* pinch of salt
* 1 cup milk
  scant ½ cup water
* 1 extra-large egg
* 2 tbsp melted butter
  1 tbsp finely chopped dill
  sunflower oil, for greasing
  lemon wedges, to serve

Filling
2 ripe avocados

2 tbsp lemon juice

12 oz/350 g cooked, peeled jumbo shrimp

salt and pepper

Cornmeal Waffles with Parsley Butter

1. For the parsley butter, beat the butter until softened, then stir in the parsley with pepper to taste.

2. Sift the flour, cornmeal, baking powder, and salt into a bowl. Add the milk, yogurt, egg, and butter and beat to a smooth batter. Stir in the corn kernels and let stand for 5 minutes.

3. Lightly grease a large waffle maker and heat until hot. Pour the batter into the waffle maker and cook until golden brown. Repeat, using the remaining batter, while keeping the cooked waffles warm.

4. Serve, with a generous spoonful of parsley butter.

Serves 4

* 1¼ cups all-purpose white flour
  scant ½ cup medium cornmeal
* 1½ tsp baking powder
* pinch of salt
* 1 cup milk
  2 tbsp plain yogurt
* 1 extra-large egg
* 2 tbsp melted butter
  7 oz/200 g canned corn kernels, drained
  sunflower oil, for greasing

Parsley butter
7 tbsp butter
3 tbsp finely chopped parsley
pepper

18

Crespolini

1. Sift the flour and salt into a bowl. Add the milk, water, egg, and oil and beat to a smooth, bubbly batter. Let stand for 15 minutes.

2. Preheat the oven to 400°F/200°C. Lightly grease a shallow ovenproof dish.

3. Grease an 8-inch/20-cm skillet and heat over medium heat. Pour in enough batter to just cover the skillet, swirling to cover in a thin, even layer. Cook until the underside is golden, then flip or turn with a spatula or palette knife and cook the other side until golden brown.

4. Repeat this process, using the remaining batter. Interleave the cooked crepes with paper towels and keep warm.

5. For the filling, mix the ricotta cheese, spinach, nutmeg, and 1 tablespoon of the Parmesan cheese and season to taste with salt and pepper. Lay a slice of ham on each crepe, then divide the cheese-and-spinach mixture between the crepes and roll up.

6. Arrange the crepes side by side in the prepared dish, brush with oil, and sprinkle with the remaining Parmesan cheese. Bake in the preheated oven for 15–20 minutes, until golden brown and bubbling. Serve hot.

Serves 4

* 1¼ cups all-purpose white flour
* pinch of salt
* 1 cup milk
  scant ½ cup water
* 1 extra-large egg
* 2 tbsp olive oil
  sunflower oil, for greasing

Filling
1 cup ricotta cheese
2¼ cups well-drained cooked spinach
½ tsp grated nutmeg
1 cup grated Parmesan cheese
8 thin slices lean cooked ham
salt and pepper

Pancakes with Baked Mushrooms

1. For the topping, preheat the oven to 400°F/ 200°C. Beat the butter until softened, stir in the parsley and chives, and season to taste with salt and pepper.

2. Mix the garlic and oil together. Place the mushrooms on a baking sheet in a single layer, brush with the garlic oil, and sprinkle with salt and pepper to taste. Bake in the oven for about 15 minutes, turning once, until tender.

3. Meanwhile, sift the flour, baking powder, and salt into a bowl. Add the milk, egg, and butter and beat to a smooth batter. Let stand for 5 minutes.

4. Lightly grease a griddle pan or skillet and heat over medium heat. Spoon tablespoons of batter into the pan and cook until bubbles appear on the surface.

5. Turn over with a spatula or palette knife and cook the other side until golden brown. Repeat this process, using the remaining batter, while keeping the cooked pancakes warm.

6. Place a mushroom on each pancake, top with a spoonful of herb butter, and serve immediately.

Serves 6

* 1¼ cups all-purpose white flour
* 1½ tsp baking powder
* pinch of salt
* 1 cup milk
* 1 extra-large egg
* 2 tbsp melted butter
  sunflower oil, for greasing

Topping
4 tbsp butter
2 tbsp chopped parsley
1 tbsp chopped chives
1 garlic clove, crushed
3 tbsp olive oil
12 portobello mushrooms
salt and pepper

20

Waffles with Crabmeat Topping

1. For the topping, combine the crabmeat, scallions, lime rind and juice, cilantro, and cayenne pepper. Spoon over the oil and lightly toss together, adding salt and pepper to taste.

2. Sift the flour, baking powder, and salt into a bowl. Add the milk, egg, butter, and cilantro and beat to a smooth batter. Let stand for 5 minutes.

3. Lightly grease a large waffle maker and heat. Pour the batter into the waffle maker and cook until golden brown. Repeat this process, using the remaining batter, while keeping the cooked waffles warm.

4. Spoon the crabmeat topping onto the waffles, drizzle with a little oil, and serve immediately.

Serves 4

* 1¼ cups all-purpose white flour
* 1½ tsp baking powder
* pinch of salt
* 1 cup milk
* 1 large egg
* 2 tbsp melted butter
  2 tbsp chopped fresh cilantro
  sunflower oil, for greasing

Topping
1 lb/450 g dressed crabmeat
4 scallions, thinly sliced diagonally
finely grated rind and juice of 1 lime
2 tbsp chopped fresh cilantro
pinch of cayenne pepper
1 tbsp olive oil, plus extra to serve
salt and pepper

Everyday

21

Caramelized Apple Pancakes

1. Sift the flour, baking powder, salt, and sugar into a bowl. Add the milk, egg, butter, and vanilla extract and beat to a smooth batter. Let stand for 5 minutes.

2. Lightly grease a griddle pan or skillet and heat over medium heat. Spoon tablespoons of batter into the pan and cook until bubbles appear on the surface.

3. Turn over with a spatula or palette knife and cook the other side until golden brown. Repeat this process, using the remaining batter, while keeping the cooked pancakes warm.

4. For the topping, melt the butter in a medium saucepan over medium heat, then add the apples. Sprinkle with sugar and fry, stirring, for 6–8 minutes, or until softened and golden brown. Stir in the nutmeg.

5. Spoon the apples and juices over the pancakes and serve immediately.

Serves 4

* 1¼ cups all-purpose white flour
* 1½ tsp baking powder
* pinch of salt
  1 tbsp superfine sugar
* 1 cup milk
* 1 extra-large egg
* 2 tbsp melted butter
  1 tsp vanilla extract
  sunflower oil, for greasing

Topping
5 tbsp butter
3 crisp apples, cored and sliced
¼ cup superfine sugar
½ tsp ground nutmeg

Peanut Butter & Jelly Waffle Sandwich

1. Sift the flour, baking powder, sugar, and salt into a bowl. Add the milk, egg, and butter and beat to a smooth batter. Let stand for 5 minutes.

2. Lightly grease a waffle maker and heat until hot. Pour the batter into the waffle maker and cook until golden brown. Repeat this process, using the remaining batter, while keeping the cooked waffles warm.

3. Spread half of the waffles with peanut butter and the remainder with jelly. Sandwich the two together with the peanut butter and jelly inside.

4. Dust with confectioners' sugar and serve immediately.

Serves 4

* 1¼ cups all-purpose white flour
* 1½ tsp baking powder
* 1 tbsp superfine sugar
* pinch of salt
* 1 cup milk
* 1 extra-large egg
* 2 tbsp melted butter
* sunflower oil, for greasing

Filling

4 tbsp chunky peanut butter

4 tbsp strawberry jelly or raspberry jelly

confectioners' sugar, for dusting

Chocolate Chip Pancakes

1. Sift the flour, baking powder, sugar, and salt into a bowl. Add the milk, egg, and butter and beat to a smooth batter. Stir in ½ cup of the chocolate chips and let stand for 5 minutes.

2. Lightly grease a griddle pan or skillet and heat over medium heat. Spoon tablespoons of batter into the pan and cook until bubbles appear on the surface.

3. Turn over with a spatula or palette knife and cook the other side until golden brown. Repeat this process, using the remaining batter, while keeping the cooked pancakes warm.

4. Place the remaining chocolate chips in a heatproof bowl and melt over a saucepan of barely simmering water (do not let the bottom of the bowl touch the water).

5. Stack the pancakes on plates, drizzle with the melted chocolate, and serve immediately.

Serves 4

- ✳ 1¼ cups all-purpose white flour
- ✳ 1½ tsp baking powder
- 1 tbsp dark brown sugar
- ✳ pinch of salt
- ✳ 1 cup milk
- ✳ 1 extra-large egg
- ✳ 2 tbsp melted butter
- ¾ cup chocolate chips
- sunflower oil, for greasing

Sweet Carrot Pancakes

1. Sift the two types of flour, baking powder, sugar, allspice, and salt into a bowl, tipping in any bran left in the sifter. Add the milk, egg, and butter and beat to a smooth batter. Stir in the carrots and raisins and let stand for 5 minutes.

2. Lightly grease a griddle pan or skillet and heat over medium heat. Spoon tablespoons of batter into the pan and cook until bubbles appear on the surface.

3. Turn over with a spatula or palette knife and cook the other side until golden brown. Repeat this process, using the remaining batter, while keeping the cooked pancakes warm.

4. Sprinkle the pancakes with sugar and serve immediately with melted butter.

Serves 4

⅔ cup all-purpose white flour
⅔ cup whole wheat flour
1½ tsp baking powder
1 tbsp dark brown sugar
1 tsp ground allspice
pinch of salt
1 cup milk
1 extra-large egg
2 tbsp melted butter
1¾ cups finely grated carrots
⅓ cup raisins
oil, for greasing
melted butter and dark brown sugar, to serve

25

English Pancakes

1. Sift the flour and salt into a bowl. Add the milk, water, egg, and butter and beat to a smooth, bubbly batter. Let stand for 15 minutes.

2. Grease an 8-inch/20-cm skillet with butter and heat over medium heat. Pour in enough batter to just cover the skillet, swirling to cover in a thin, even layer. Cook until the underside is golden, then turn with a spatula or palette knife and cook the other side until golden brown.

3. Repeat this process, using the remaining batter. Interleave the cooked pancakes with paper towels and keep warm.

4. Dust each pancake with sugar, then sprinkle with lemon juice, roll up, and serve immediately.

Serves 4

* 1¼ cups all-purpose white flour
* pinch of salt
* 1 cup milk
  scant ½ cup water
* 1 extra-large egg
* 2 tbsp melted butter
  butter, for frying
  superfine sugar and lemon
  juice, to serve

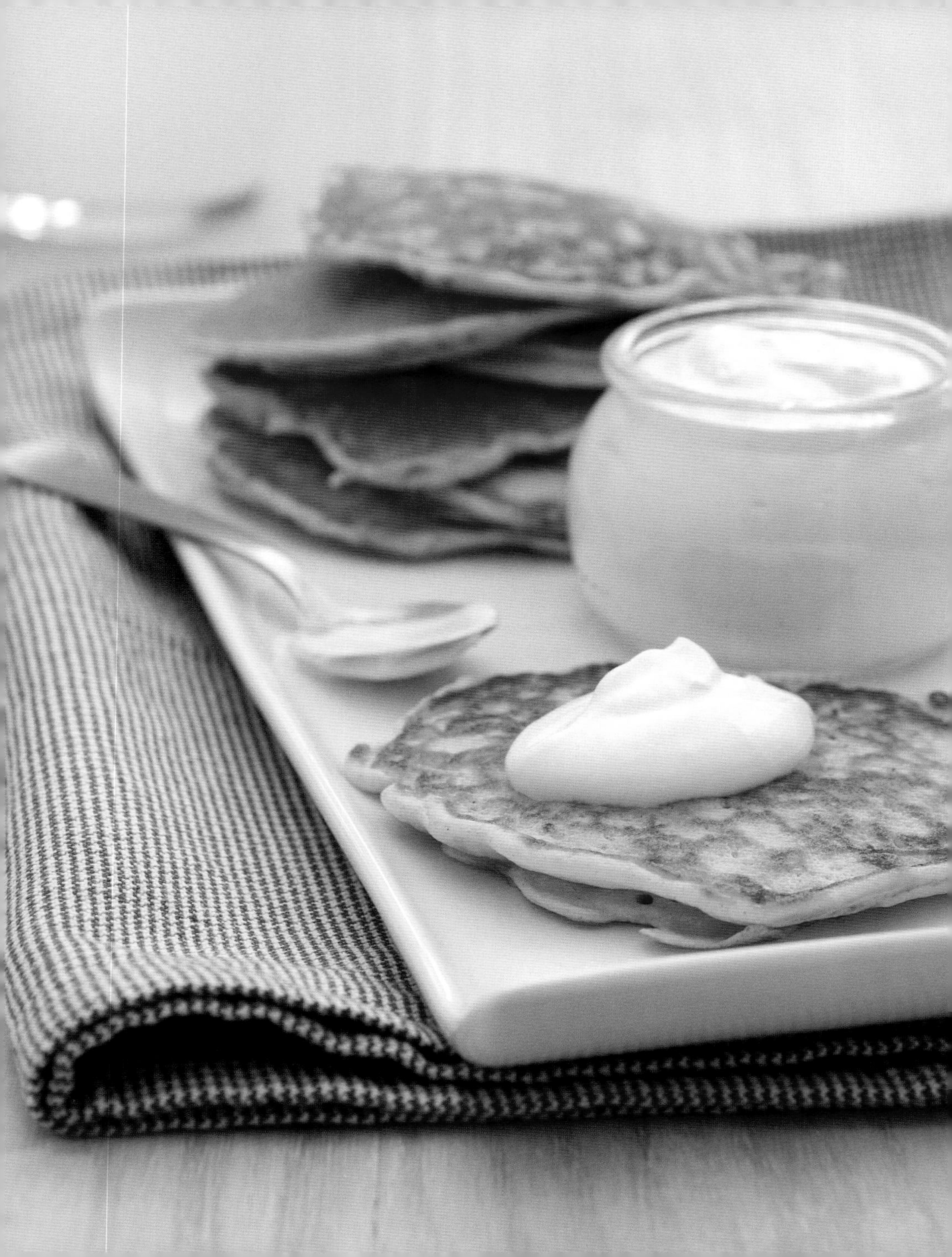

Potato & Chive Pancakes

1. Sift the flour, baking powder, and salt into a bowl. Add the milk, egg, and oil and beat to a smooth batter.

2. Peel the potatoes and grate coarsely, then place in a colander or strainer and sprinkle with salt. Let stand for 5 minutes, then press out as much liquid as possible. Stir the grated potato into the batter with the chives, mustard, and pepper to taste.

3. Lightly grease a griddle pan or skillet and heat over medium heat. Spoon tablespoons of batter into the pan and cook until bubbles appear on the surface.

4. Turn over with a spatula or palette knife and cook the other side until golden brown. Repeat this process, using the remaining batter, while keeping the cooked pancakes warm.

5. Serve immediately, with a spoonful of yogurt.

Serves 4

* 1¼ cups all-purpose white flour
* 1½ tsp baking powder
* pinch of salt
* 1 cup milk
* 1 extra-large egg
* 2 tbsp sunflower oil, plus extra for greasing
* 2 potatoes
* 2 tbsp chopped chives
* 1 tbsp whole-grain mustard
* pepper
* Greek-style yogurt or sour cream, to serve

Polenta Waffles with Roasted Cherry Tomatoes

1. For the topping, preheat the oven to 425°F/220°C. Arrange the tomatoes on a baking sheet, drizzle with oil, and season to taste with salt and pepper. Roast in the preheated oven for about 10 minutes, until tender and lightly browned.

2. Meanwhile, sift the flour, polenta, baking powder, and salt into a bowl. Add the buttermilk, egg, and oil and beat to a smooth batter. Let stand for 5 minutes.

3. Lightly grease a waffle maker and heat until hot. Pour the batter into the waffle maker and cook in batches until golden brown, while keeping the cooked waffles warm.

4. Top the waffles with the tomatoes, sprinkle with balsamic vinegar, and serve immediately.

Serves 4

- 1¼ cups all-purpose white flour
- ⅓ cup instant polenta
- 1½ tsp baking powder
- pinch of salt
- 1 cup buttermilk
- 1 extra-large egg
- 2 tbsp olive oil
- sunflower oil, for greasing

Topping
12 oz/350 g cherry tomatoes
2 tbsp olive oil
salt and pepper
balsamic vinegar, to serve

28

Cheese & Bacon Waffles

1. Preheat the broiler to high. Place the bacon on a broiler rack and broil for 3–4 minutes, turning once, until golden brown and crisp. Drain on paper towels, then crumble or chop into small pieces.

2. Sift the flour, baking powder, and salt into a bowl. Add the milk, egg, and butter and beat to a smooth batter. Stir in the bacon and cheese and let stand for 5 minutes.

3. Lightly grease a waffle maker and heat until hot. Pour the batter into the waffle maker and cook until golden brown. Repeat, using the remaining batter, while keeping the cooked waffles warm.

4. Sprinkle the waffles with grated cheese and serve immediately.

Serves 4

2 slices bacon
* 1¼ cups all-purpose white flour
* 1½ tsp baking powder
* pinch of salt
* 1 cup milk
* 1 extra-large egg
* 2 tbsp melted butter
¾ cup finely grated cheddar cheese, plus extra for sprinkling
sunflower oil, for greasing

29

Crispy Crepes with Ratatouille

1. For the filling, heat the oil in a large skillet over medium heat, add the onion and eggplant, and fry until golden. Add the garlic, zucchini, tomatoes, and oregano and season to taste with salt and pepper. Cover and simmer for 25–30 minutes, or until tender.

2. Meanwhile, sift the two types of flour and the salt into a bowl, tipping in any bran left in the sifter. Add the milk, water, egg, and olive oil and beat to a smooth, bubbly batter. Let stand for 15 minutes.

3. Grease an 8-inch/20-cm skillet and heat over medium heat. Pour in enough batter to just cover the skillet, swirling to cover in a thin, even layer. Cook until the underside is golden, then flip or turn with a spatula or palette knife and cook the other side until golden.

4. Repeat this process, using the remaining batter. Interleave the cooked crepes with paper towels and keep warm.

5. Preheat the oven to 400°F/200°C and grease a wide ovenproof dish.

6. Spoon the filling onto one side of each crepe and fold over the other side. Arrange in the prepared dish in one layer, brush with oil, and sprinkle with breadcrumbs. Bake for 25–30 minutes, until golden. Serve immediately.

Serves 4

⅔ cup all-purpose white flour
⅔ cup whole wheat flour
pinch of salt
1 cup milk
½ cup water
1 extra-large egg
2 tbsp olive oil
sunflower oil, for greasing
4 tbsp dry whole wheat breadcrumbs

Filling
3 tbsp olive oil
1 red onion, diced
1 large eggplant, diced
1 garlic clove, crushed
1 large zucchini, diced
14 oz/400 g canned chopped tomatoes
2 tbsp chopped fresh oregano
salt and pepper

Crepe Fajitas

1. For the filling, place the steak in a bowl and add the garlic, coriander, cumin, chili powder, lime, and 1 tablespoon of the oil. Cover and let chill in the refrigerator for 30 minutes.

2. Sift the cornmeal, cornstarch, and salt into a bowl. Add the milk, water, egg, and oil and beat to a smooth batter. Let stand for 15 minutes.

3. Lightly grease an 8-inch/20-cm skillet and heat over medium heat. Stir the batter and pour in enough to just cover the skillet, swirling to cover evenly. Cook until the underside is golden, then flip or turn with a spatula or palette knife and cook the other side until golden.

4. Repeat this process, using the remaining batter. Interleave the cooked crepes with paper towels and keep warm.

5. To complete the filling, heat the remaining olive oil in a large skillet over medium heat, add the red and yellow bell peppers and onion and fry for 2–3 minutes to soften. Add the steak strips and stir-fry for an additional 3–4 minutes, until golden.

6. Spoon the filling onto the crepes, season to taste with salt and pepper, and add a spoonful of sour cream and a spoonful of grated cheese to each. Fold over and serve immediately.

Serves 4

1 cup medium cornmeal
2 tbsp cornstarch
pinch of salt
1 cup milk
scant ½ cup water
1 extra-large egg
2 tbsp corn oil, plus extra for greasing

Filling
1 lb 5 oz/600 g sirloin steak or flank steak, cut into thin strips
2 garlic cloves, crushed
2 tsp ground coriander
1 tsp ground cumin
1 tsp chili powder
juice of 1 lime
3 tbsp olive oil
1 red bell pepper, seeded and sliced
1 yellow bell pepper, seeded and sliced
1 large red onion
salt and pepper
sour cream and grated cheddar cheese, to serve

31

Quick Chicken & Pesto Roll Ups

1. Sift the flour and salt into a bowl. Add the milk, tomato juice, egg, oil, and pesto and beat to a smooth batter. Let stand for 15 minutes.

2. Meanwhile, for the filling, place the chicken, tomatoes, and pesto in a medium saucepan and heat gently over medium heat, until boiling. Remove from the heat, stir in the mayonnaise, and keep warm while making the crepes.

3. Lightly grease an 8-inch/20-cm skillet and heat over medium heat. Pour in enough batter to just cover the skillet, swirling to cover in a thin, even layer. Cook until the underside is golden, then flip or turn with a spatula or palette knife and cook the other side until golden brown.

4. Repeat this process, using the remaining batter. Interleave the cooked crepes with paper towels and keep warm.

5. Spoon the chicken filling onto the crepes and roll up firmly. Cut into thick slices diagonally and serve immediately with a green salad.

Serves 4

* 1¼ cups all-purpose white flour
* pinch of salt
* 1 cup milk
  scant ½ cup tomato juice
* 1 extra-large egg
* 2 tbsp olive oil, plus extra for greasing
  2 tbsp green pesto
  green salad, to serve

Filling
3¼ cups diced, cooked chicken
3 tomatoes, diced
2 tbsp green pesto
3 tbsp mayonnaise

Cannelloni Crepes

1. Sift the flour and salt into a bowl. Add the milk, water, egg, and 2 tablespoons of the olive oil and beat to a smooth batter. Let stand for 15 minutes.

2. Lightly grease an 8-inch/20-cm skillet and heat over medium heat. Pour in enough batter to just cover the skillet, swirling to cover in an even layer. Cook until the underside is golden, then flip or turn with a spatula or palette knife and cook the other side until golden brown.

3. Repeat this process, using the remaining batter. Interleave the cooked crepes with paper towels and keep warm.

4. For the filling, heat 2 tablespoons of the olive oil in a skillet over medium heat, then add the onion and fry for 2–3 minutes, until softened. Add the turkey and stir-fry for 4–5 minutes, until lightly browned. Add the tomatoes, season to taste with salt and pepper, cover, and simmer for 15 minutes. Add the basil.

5. Preheat the oven to 400°F/200°C. Grease a wide ovenproof dish. Fold in about 1 inch/2.5 cm on opposite sides of each crepe. Divide the filling among the crepes, then roll up and arrange in a single layer in the prepared dish, spooning over the juices.

6. Brush with the remaining olive oil, sprinkle with cheese, and bake in the preheated oven for 25–30 minutes, until golden. Serve immediately.

Serves 4

* 1¼ cups all-purpose white flour
* pinch of salt
* 1 cup milk
  4 tbsp water
* 1 extra-large egg
  3 tbsp olive oil
  sunflower oil, for greasing
  ⅓ cup freshly grated Parmesan cheese

Filling
3 tbsp olive oil
1 large onion, sliced
1 lb 2 oz/500 g ground turkey
14 oz/400 g canned chopped tomatoes
3 tbsp chopped fresh basil
salt and pepper

Scallion Pancakes with Mushrooms & Goat Cheese

1. Sift the flour, baking powder, and salt into a bowl. Add the milk, egg, and butter and beat to a smooth batter. Stir in the chopped scallions and let stand for 5 minutes.

2. Lightly grease a griddle pan or skillet and heat over medium heat. Spoon 2 tablespoons of batter into the pan and cook until bubbles appear on the surface.

3. Turn over with a spatula or palette knife and cook the other side until golden brown. Repeat this process, using the remaining batter, while keeping the cooked pancakes warm.

4. For the topping, melt the butter in a skillet over medium heat, then add the shallots and fry for 2 minutes, until softened. Add the mushrooms and thyme and cook, stirring frequently, until golden. Season to taste with salt and pepper.

5. Spoon the mushrooms onto the pancakes and top with pieces of cheese. Serve immediately, garnished with sprigs of thyme.

Serves 4

* 1¼ cups all-purpose white flour
* 1½ tsp baking powder
* pinch of salt
* 1 cup milk
* 1 extra-large egg
* 2 tbsp melted butter

8 scallions, finely chopped

sunflower oil, for greasing

Topping
2 tbsp butter

2 shallots, finely chopped

12 oz/350 g closed cup mushrooms, quartered

1 tbsp chopped fresh thyme, plus extra sprigs to garnish

4½ oz/125 g goat cheese

salt and pepper

Cheese & Onion Waffles with Apple & Onion Salsa

1. For the salsa, heat the oil in a skillet over medium heat, add the onions and sugar, and cook, stirring occasionally, for 20 minutes, or until soft and golden. Add the apples, crushed pepper, and vinegar and simmer for an additional 15 minutes. Let cool.

2. Sift the flour, baking powder, and salt into a bowl. Add the milk, egg, and butter and beat to a smooth batter. Stir in the cheese and onion and let stand for 5 minutes.

3. Lightly grease a waffle maker and heat until hot. Pour the batter into the waffle maker and cook until golden brown. Repeat, using the remaining batter, while keeping the cooked waffles warm.

4. Serve immediately, with a generous spoonful of the salsa.

Serves 4

- 1¼ cups all-purpose white flour
- 1½ tsp baking powder
- pinch of salt
- 1 cup milk
- 1 extra-large egg
- 2 tbsp melted butter
- ¾ cup grated cheddar cheese
- 1 red onion, coarsely grated
- sunflower oil, for greasing

Apple & onion salsa
- 2 tbsp olive oil
- 350 g/12 oz red onions, diced
- 3 tbsp packed dark brown sugar
- 2 apples, peeled, cored, and diced
- ¼ tsp crushed red pepper
- 2 tbsp cider vinegar

Parmesan Crepe Wraps with Spinach & Walnuts

1. Sift the flour and salt into a bowl. Add the milk, water, egg, and butter and beat to a smooth batter. Stir in the cheese and let stand for 15 minutes.

2. Lightly grease an 8-inch/20-cm skillet and heat over medium heat. Beat the batter lightly and pour in enough to just cover the skillet, swirling to cover in a thin, even layer. Cook until the underside is golden, then flip or turn with a spatula or palette knife and cook the other side until golden brown.

3. Repeat this process, using the remaining batter. Interleave the cooked crepes with paper towels and keep warm.

4. For the filling, place the spinach, celery, apple, and walnuts in a bowl and toss together. Whisk together the oil, vinegar, and salt and pepper to taste and toss into the salad.

5. Divide the salad among the crepes, fold over, and serve immediately.

Serves 4

- 1¼ cups all-purpose white flour
- pinch of salt
- 1 cup milk
- 4 tbsp water
- 1 extra-large egg
- 2 tbsp melted butter
- ⅓ cup finely grated Parmesan cheese
- sunflower oil, for greasing

Filling
- 3½ oz/100 g baby spinach leaves
- 2 stalks celery, chopped
- 1 apple, thinly sliced
- ½ cup chopped walnuts
- 2 tbsp walnut oil
- 1 tbsp white wine vinegar
- salt and pepper

Sweet Potato Waffles with Frankfurters

1. For the topping, melt the butter with the oil in a large skillet over medium heat, then add the onions and cook gently for about 10 minutes, stirring frequently, until softened. Stir in the sugar and cook for an additional 5–10 minutes, until golden brown. Remove from the heat and keep hot.

2. Bring a saucepan of lightly salted water to the boil, add the sweet potato, and cook for 10–15 minutes, or until tender. Drain thoroughly, then mash until smooth. Let cool.

3. Sift the flour, baking powder, and salt into a bowl. Add the milk, egg, and oil and beat to a smooth batter. Stir in the sweet potato and season to taste with pepper. Let stand for 5 minutes.

4. Lightly grease a waffle maker and heat until hot. Pour the batter into the waffle maker and cook, until golden brown. Repeat, using the remaining batter, while keeping the cooked waffles warm.

5. Preheat a broiler to high, place the frankfurters on a broiler rack, and broil for 5–6 minutes, turning frequently. Remove from the broiler and slice.

6. Spoon the frankfurters and onions over the waffles and serve immediately.

Serves 4

- 1⅔ cups peeled and cubed sweet potato
- 1¼ cups all-purpose white flour
- 1½ tsp baking powder
- pinch of salt
- 1 cup milk
- 1 extra-large egg
- 2 tbsp sunflower oil, plus extra for greasing
- pepper

Topping
- 2 tbsp butter
- 1 tbsp sunflower oil
- 3 onions, thinly sliced
- 1 tbsp raw brown sugar
- 8 frankfurters

37

Eggplant, Bell Pepper & Basil Crepe Rolls

1. For the filling, slice the eggplants lengthwise into ⅜-inch/ 8-mm-thick slices, sprinkle with salt, and let drain for about 20 minutes. Rinse and dry.

2. Preheat the broiler to high. Arrange the eggplant slices on a baking sheet in a single layer, brush with olive oil, and broil until golden, turning once. Arrange the red bell peppers, cut side down, on a baking sheet in a single layer and broil until blackened. Remove the skins and slice.

3. Sift the flour and salt into a bowl. Add the milk, water, egg, and oil and beat to a smooth, bubbly batter. Let stand for 15 minutes.

4. Lightly grease an 8-inch/20-cm skillet and heat over medium heat. Pour in enough batter to just cover the skillet, swirling to cover in a thin, even layer. Cook until the underside is golden, then flip or turn with a spatula or palette knife and cook the other side until golden brown.

5. Repeat this process, using the remaining batter. Interleave the cooked crepes with paper towels and keep warm.

6. Arrange the pancakes in pairs, slightly overlapping. Spread with cheese and top with the eggplants, red bell peppers, basil, and salt and pepper to taste. Roll up firmly from one short side. Cut in half diagonally and serve immediately.

Serves 4

* 1¼ cups all-purpose white flour
* pinch of salt
* 1 cup milk
  scant ½ cup water
* 1 extra-large egg
* 2 tbsp olive oil
  sunflower oil, for greasing

Filling
2 large eggplants
olive oil, for brushing
2 large red bell peppers, halved and seeded
generous 1 cup cream cheese
handful of fresh basil leaves
salt and pepper

Crepe Tagliatelle with Seafood Sauce

1. Sift the flour and salt into a bowl. Add the milk, water, egg, and oil and whisk to a smooth, bubbly batter. Let stand for 15 minutes.

2. Lightly grease an 8-inch/20-cm skillet and heat over medium heat. Pour in enough batter to just cover the skillet, swirling to cover in a fairly thin, even layer. Cook until the underside is golden, then flip or turn with a spatula or palette knife and cook the other side until golden brown.

3. Repeat this process, using the remaining batter. Interleave the cooked crepes with paper towels and keep warm. When you have used all the batter, roll up the crepes and cut into ½-inch/1-cm-thick slices.

4. For the sauce, melt the butter in a large skillet over medium heat, then add the shallots and fry for 3–4 minutes, until softened. Add the mussels, shrimp, and lemon juice and stir until thoroughly heated. Stir in the crème fraîche and season to taste with salt and pepper.

5. Heat the sauce until almost boiling, then add the sliced crepes and lightly toss to mix. Sprinkle with the parsley and lemon zest and serve immediately.

Serves 4

* 1¼ cups all-purpose white flour
* pinch of salt
* 1 cup milk
  4 tbsp water
* 1 extra-large egg
* 2 tbsp sunflower oil, plus extra for greasing
  chopped parsley and lemon zest, to garnish

Seafood sauce
1 tbsp butter
2 shallots, thinly sliced
9 oz/250 g cooked, shelled mussels
9 oz/250 g cooked, peeled shrimp
juice of 1 lemon
¾ cup crème fraîche or sour cream
salt and pepper

Tomato & Zucchini Crepe Layer

1. Sift the flour and salt into a bowl. Add the milk, water, egg, and butter and beat to a smooth, bubbly batter. Let stand for 15 minutes.

2. Lightly grease an 8-inch/20-cm skillet and heat over medium heat. Pour in enough batter to just cover the skillet, swirling to cover in a fairly thin, even layer. Cook until the underside is golden, then flip or turn with a spatula or palette knife and cook the other side until golden brown.

3. Repeat this process, using the remaining batter. Interleave the cooked crepes with paper towels and keep warm.

4. For the filling, preheat the oven to 375°F/190°C. Heat the oil in a skillet over medium heat, then add the onions, zucchini, and garlic and fry, stirring, for 2–3 minutes, until softened.

5. Place one crepe on a baking sheet and top with a layer of onions, zucchini, garlic, tomatoes, cheese, and salt and pepper to taste. Continue to layer the remaining crepes and vegetables to make a large stack.

6. Brush the top of the stack with butter, add a few pieces of cheese, and bake in the preheated oven for about 30 minutes, until thoroughly heated. Slice into wedges and serve immediately.

Serves 4

* 1¼ cups all-purpose white flour
* pinch of salt
* 1 cup milk
  scant ½ cup water
* 1 extra-large egg
* 2 tbsp melted butter, plus extra for greasing

Filling
2 tbsp olive oil
1 onion, sliced
3 zucchini, sliced
2 garlic cloves, crushed
4 large tomatoes, sliced
2 cups chopped mozzarella cheese, plus extra for topping
salt and pepper

40

Waffle Open Sandwich with Duck & Hoisin Sauce

1 For the topping, remove the skin from the duck and cut the meat into thin strips. Heat the oil in a wok over medium heat, then add the duck and stir-fry for about 3 minutes, until evenly colored. Add the hoisin sauce and simmer gently for 2 minutes. Keep warm.

2 Sift the flour, baking powder, and salt into a bowl. Add the milk, egg, oil, and five-spice paste and beat to a smooth batter. Let stand for 5 minutes.

3 Lightly grease a waffle maker and heat until hot. Pour the batter into the waffle maker and cook until golden brown. Repeat, using the remaining batter, while keeping the cooked waffles warm.

4 Top the waffles with the scallions, cucumber, and duck, spoon over the sauce, and serve immediately.

Serves 4

* 1¼ cups all-purpose white flour
* 1½ tsp baking powder
* pinch of salt
* 1 cup milk
* 1 extra-large egg
* 2 tbsp sunflower oil, plus extra for greasing
  1 tsp Chinese five-spice paste

Topping
2 large duck breasts, about 12 oz/350 g each
1 tbsp sesame oil
scant ½ cup hoisin sauce
1 bunch scallions, cut into matchsticks
½ cucumber, seeded and cut into matchsticks

Indulgent

41

Brownie Waffles

1. Sift the flour, baking powder, salt, baking soda, cocoa, sugar, and cinnamon into a bowl. Add the milk, egg, butter, cream, and vanilla extract and beat to a smooth batter. Stir in the chocolate chips and nuts and let stand for 5 minutes.

2. Lightly grease a waffle maker and heat until hot. Pour the batter into the waffle maker and cook until crisp and browned. Repeat, using the remaining batter, while keeping the cooked waffles warm.

3. Serve immediately, topped with the cream and sprinkled with a few nuts.

Serves 4

* 1¼ cups all-purpose white flour
* 1½ tsp baking powder
* pinch of salt
  ½ tsp baking soda
  ¼ cup unsweetened cocoa
  ¼ cup superfine sugar
  1 tsp ground cinnamon
* 1 cup milk
* 1 extra-large egg
* 2 tbsp melted butter
  3 tbsp heavy cream
  1 tsp vanilla extract
  ½ cup chocolate chips
  ⅓ cup chopped pecans, plus extra to decorate
  sunflower oil, for greasing
  heavy cream, whipped, to serve

Butterscotch Waffles Ice Cream Stack

1. For the sauce, place the sugar, butter, cream, and brandy, if using, in a small saucepan over low heat and stir until melted. Bring to a boil, stirring, then remove from the heat and keep warm.

2. Sift the flour, baking powder, salt, and sugar into a bowl. Add the milk, egg, and butter and beat to a smooth batter. Let stand for 5 minutes.

3. Lightly grease a waffle maker and heat until hot. Pour the batter into the waffle maker and cook until golden brown. Repeat, using the remaining batter, while keeping the cooked waffles warm.

4. Spoon the butterscotch sauce over the waffles and serve immediately with scoops of vanilla ice cream.

Serves 4

- 1¼ cups all-purpose white flour
- 1½ tsp baking powder
- pinch of salt
- 2 tbsp dark brown sugar
- 1 cup milk
- 1 extra-large egg
- 2 tbsp melted butter
- sunflower oil, for greasing

Butterscotch sauce
- ⅓ cup packed dark brown sugar
- 4 tbp unsalted butter
- 4 tbsp heavy cream
- 1 tbsp brandy (optional)
- vanilla ice cream, to serve

Double Chocolate Crepes

1. Sift the flour and salt into a bowl. Add the milk, water, egg, and butter and beat to a smooth, bubbly batter.

2. Pour ⅔ cup of batter into a pitcher and whisk in the cocoa and cream. Pour the remaining batter into a separate pitcher. Let both batters stand for 15 minutes.

3. Grease an 8-inch/20-cm skillet and heat over medium heat. Pouring from the two separate pitchers, swirl the two colors of batter together to just cover the skillet, covering in a fairly thin, even layer.

4. Cook until the underside is golden, then flip or turn with a spatula or palette knife and cook the other side until golden brown.

5. Repeat this process, using the remaining batter. Interleave the cooked crepes with paper towels and keep warm.

6. For the filling, put the white chocolate, cream, and vanilla extract into a small saucepan over low heat and stir, without boiling, until the chocolate is melted.

7. Pour a little of the white chocolate cream onto each crepe, fold over, top with a scattering of grated chocolate, and serve immediately.

Serves 4

* 1¼ cups all-purpose white flour
* pinch of salt
* 1 cup milk
* ½ cup water
* 1 extra-large egg
* 2 tbsp melted butter
* 2 tbsp unsweetened cocoa
* 3 tbsp light cream
* butter, for greasing

Filling
5 oz/140 g white chocolate
⅔ cup light cream
1 tsp vanilla extract
3 tbsp coarsely grated
   semisweet dark chocolate

Chocolate-Dipped Waffles

1. Sift the flour, baking powder, salt, and sugar into a bowl. Add the cream, water, egg, butter, and vanilla extract and beat to a smooth batter. Let stand for 5 minutes.

2. Lightly grease a waffle maker and heat until hot. Pour the batter into the waffle maker and cook until golden brown. Repeat, using the remaining batter, while keeping the cooked waffles warm.

3. Place the chocolate in a bowl over a saucepan of just simmering water and heat very gently until just melted (do not let the bottom of the bowl touch the water). Dip the waffles into the chocolate, spooning it over to coat them halfway. Place the waffles on a sheet of nonstick parchment paper and let rest until the chocolate is just set. Serve immediately.

Serves 4

- ※ 1¼ cups all-purpose white flour
- ※ 1½ tsp baking powder
- ※ pinch of salt
  2 tbsp dark brown sugar
- ※ 1 cup light cream
  1 tbsp water
- ※ 1 extra-large egg
- ※ 2 tbsp melted butter
  1 tsp vanilla extract
  sunflower oil, for greasing
  14 oz/400 g semisweet dark chocolate, for dipping

45

Sugar Plum Pancakes

1. For the topping, cut the plums into wedges. Melt the butter in a wide saucepan over high heat, then add the plums and fry for 2–3 minutes. Stir in the sugar and cook over medium heat, stirring occasionally, until syrupy and slightly caramelized.

2. Sift the flour, baking powder, salt, sugar, and ginger into a bowl. Add the cream, water, egg, and butter and beat to a smooth batter. Let stand for 5 minutes.

3. Lightly grease a griddle pan or skillet and heat over medium heat. Spoon tablespoons of batter into the pan and cook until bubbles appear on the surface.

4. Turn over with a spatula palette knife and cook the other side until golden brown. Repeat this process, using the remaining batter, while keeping the cooked pancakes warm.

5. Serve warm, with the plums and syrup spooned over.

Serves 4

- 1¼ cups all-purpose white flour
- 1½ tsp baking powder
- pinch of salt
- 1 tbsp superfine sugar
- 1 tsp ground ginger
- 1 cup light cream
- 2 tbsp water
- 1 extra-large egg
- 2 tbsp melted butter
- sunflower oil, for greasing

Topping
1 lb 2 oz/500 g/red plums, halved and pitted
5 tbsp butter
scant ½ cup raw brown sugar

Banana Caramel Crepes

1. Sift the flour and salt into a bowl. Add the milk, coffee, egg, and butter and beat to a smooth, bubbly batter. Let stand for 15 minutes.

2. For the filling, put the condensed milk and ¼ cup of the cream into a heavy-bottom saucepan over low heat and stir until boiling. Cook over medium heat, stirring continuously, until the mixture starts to caramelize and turns a pale golden brown in color. Remove from the heat and keep warm.

3. Grease an 8-inch/20-cm skillet and heat over medium heat. Pour in enough batter to just cover the skillet, swirling to cover in a fairly thin, even layer. Cook until the underside is golden, then flip or turn with a spatula or palette knife and cook the other side until golden brown.

4. Repeat this process, using the remaining batter. Interleave the cooked crepes with paper towels and keep warm.

5. Spoon the caramel onto the crepes, slice the bananas, and arrange on top, then fold the crepes over.

6. Whip the remaining cream until just holding its shape, then spoon over the crepes, sprinkle with grated chocolate, and serve.

Serves 4

* 1¼ cups all-purpose white flour
* pinch of salt
* 1 cup milk
  scant ½ cup strong cold black coffee
* 1 extra-large egg
* 2 tbsp melted butter
  butter, for greasing

Filling
1¾ cups condensed milk
1¼ cups heavy cream
3 bananas
3 tbsp coarsely grated chocolate, to serve

Lemon Cheesecake Waffles

1. For the filling, beat the cream cheese, confectioners' sugar, lemon rind, and lemon juice together until smooth.

2. Sift the flour, baking powder, salt, superfine sugar, and ginger into a bowl. Add the milk, egg, and butter and beat to a smooth batter. Let stand for 5 minutes.

3. Lightly grease a waffle maker and heat until hot. Pour the batter into the waffle maker and cook until golden brown. Repeat, using the remaining batter, leaving the cooked waffles to cool.

4. Spread half of the waffles with the lemon cheesecake filling and sandwich together with the remainder. Top with a spoonful of crème fraîche, sprinkle with the macadamia nuts and lemon zest curls, and serve.

Serves 4

* 1¼ cups all-purpose white flour
* 1½ tsp baking powder
* pinch of salt
  2 tbsp superfine sugar
  1 tsp ground ginger
* 1 cup milk
* 1 extra-large egg
* 2 tbsp melted butter
  sunflower oil, for greasing

Filling & topping
1½ cups cream cheese
¼ cup confectioners' sugar
finely grated rind and juice of 1 lemon
4 tbsp crème fraîche or sour cream
⅓ cup chopped and toasted macadamia nuts, and curls of lemon zest, to decorate

48

Ice Cream Crepes with Berry Compote

1. Sift the flour, salt, and sugar into a bowl. Add the milk, water, egg, butter, and brandy and beat to a smooth, bubbly batter. Let stand for 15 minutes.

2. Meanwhile, for the filling, place the blueberries and raspberries in a small saucepan with the maple syrup. Heat gently until the juices run, then remove from the heat and keep warm.

3. Grease an 8-inch/20-cm skillet and heat over medium heat. Pour in enough batter to just cover the skillet, swirling to cover in a fairly thin, even layer. Cook until the underside is golden, then flip or turn with a spatula or palette knife and cook the other side until golden brown.

4. Repeat this process, using the remaining batter. Interleave the cooked crepes with paper towels and keep warm.

5. Scoop the ice cream onto the crepes and fold over. Spoon the berries and syrup on top and serve immediately.

Serves 4

* 1¼ cups all-purpose white flour
* pinch of salt
  1 tbsp confectioners' sugar
* 1 cup milk
  scant ½ cup water
* 1 extra-large egg
* 2 tbsp melted butter
  1 tbsp brandy
  butter, for greasing

Filling
⅔ cup blueberries
¾ cup raspberries
4 tbsp maple syrup
3¾ cups mixed berry ice cream
  or raspberry ice cream

49

Almond & Strawberry Pancakes

1. Sift the flour, baking powder, salt, and sugar into a bowl. Add the milk, egg, butter, cream, almonds, and almond extract and beat to a smooth batter. Let stand for 5 minutes.

2. Lightly grease a griddle pan or skillet and heat over medium heat. Spoon tablespoons of batter into the pan and cook until bubbles appear on the surface.

3. Turn over with a spatula or palette knife and cook the other side until golden brown. Repeat this process, using the remaining batter, while keeping the cooked pancakes warm.

4. Stack the pancakes in threes with crème fraîche and strawberries between. Top with a spoonful of crème fraîche and a strawberry slice, then sprinkle with confectioners' sugar and slivered almonds and serve immediately.

Serves 4

* 1¼ cups all-purpose white flour
* 1½ tsp baking powder
* pinch of salt
  2 tbsp superfine sugar
* 1 cup milk
* 1 extra-large egg
* 2 tbsp melted butter
  2 tbsp light cream
  2 tbsp ground almonds
  1 tsp almond extract
  sunflower oil, for greasing

Filling & topping
1 cup crème fraîche or vanilla yogurt
1½ cups sliced strawberries
confectioners' sugar, for dusting
3 tbsp slivered almonds, toasted, to serve

50

Pear & Peanut Butter Pancakes

1. Sift the flour, baking powder, salt, and sugar into a bowl. Add the milk, egg, oil, and peanut butter and beat to a smooth batter. Let stand for 5 minutes.

2. For the topping, place the butter and sugar in a small saucepan over low heat and heat gently, stirring until melted. Remove from the heat and keep warm.

3. Core and slice the pears and sprinkle with lemon juice to prevent them from browning.

4. Lightly grease a griddle pan or skillet and heat over medium heat. Spoon large spoonfuls of batter into the pan and cook until bubbles appear on the surface.

5. Turn over with a spatula or palette knife and cook the other side until golden brown. Repeat this process, using the remaining batter, while keeping the cooked pancakes warm.

6. Drizzle over the brown sugar syrup and serve the pancakes in twos with the sliced pears.

Serves 4

* 1¼ cups all-purpose white flour
* 1½ tsp baking powder
* pinch of salt
* 1 tbsp dark brown sugar
* 1 cup milk
* 1 extra-large egg
* 2 tbsp sunflower oil, plus extra for greasing
* 2 tbsp smooth peanut butter

Topping
2 tbp butter
3 tbsp dark brown sugar
2 ripe pears
1 tbsp lemon juice

Belgian Waffles

1. Sift the flour, baking powder, salt, and sugar into a bowl. Add the milk, egg yolks, and butter and beat to a smooth batter. Whisk the egg whites in a clean bowl until soft peaks form, then fold into the batter.

2. Lightly grease a waffle maker and heat until hot. Pour the batter into the waffle maker and cook until golden brown. Repeat, using the remaining batter, while keeping the cooked waffles warm.

3. Whip the cream until thick enough to just hold its shape and spoon into a pastry bag fitted with a large star tip. Pipe the cream onto the waffles and top with the strawberries. Dust with confectioners' sugar and serve immediately.

Serves 6

- 1¼ cups all-purpose white flour
- 1½ tsp baking powder
- pinch of salt
- 3 tbsp confectioners' sugar
- 1 cup milk
- 3 extra-large eggs, separated
- 2 tbsp melted butter
- sunflower oil, for greasing
- confectioners' sugar, for dusting

Topping
- 1¼ cups heavy cream
- 12 oz/350 g strawberries, halved if large

52

Waffle Tiramisu Stacks

1. Sift the flour, baking powder, salt, and sugar into a bowl and stir in the instant coffee. Add the milk, egg, and butter and beat to a smooth batter. Let stand for 5 minutes.

2. Lightly grease a waffle maker and heat until hot. Pour the batter into the waffle maker and cook until golden brown. Repeat, using the remaining batter, while keeping the cooked waffles warm.

3. Sprinkle the waffles with half of the liqueur and stir the rest into the mascarpone cheese. Spread half of the waffles with mascarpone cheese, then top with the remaining waffles, sprinkle with unsweetened cocoa and confectioners' sugar and serve immediately.

Serves 4

* 1¼ cups all-purpose white flour
* 1½ tsp baking powder
* pinch of salt
  1 tbsp confectioners' sugar
  1 tbsp instant coffee
* 1 cup milk
* 1 extra-large egg
* 2 tbsp melted butter
  sunflower oil, for greasing
  unsweetened cocoa and confectioners' sugar, for dusting

Filling
6 tbsp coffee liqueur
1 cup mascarpone cheese

53

Sour Cream Pecan Pancakes with Whiskey-Maple Sauce

① Sift the flour, baking powder, salt, and sugar into a bowl. Add the sour cream, milk, egg, and butter and beat to a smooth batter. Stir in the nuts and let stand for 5 minutes.

② Meanwhile, for the sauce, place the butter and maple syrup in a saucepan over low heat and heat until melted. Add the whiskey and stir until almost boiling. Remove from the heat, add the nutmeg, and keep warm.

③ Lightly grease a griddle pan or skillet and heat over medium heat. Spoon tablespoons of batter into the pan and cook until bubbles appear on the surface.

④ Turn over with a spatula or palette knife and cook the other side until golden brown. Repeat this process, using the remaining batter, while keeping the cooked pancakes warm.

⑤ Pour the sauce over the pancakes, sprinkle with the nuts, and serve immediately.

Serves 4

＊ 1¼ cups all-purpose white flour
＊ 1½ tsp baking powder
＊ pinch of salt
   2 tbsp dark brown sugar
＊ 1 cup sour cream
   2 tbsp milk
＊ 1 extra-large egg
＊ 2 tbsp melted butter
   ⅓ cup finely chopped pecans, plus extra to decorate
   sunflower oil, for greasing

Sauce
7 tbsp unsalted butter
scant ½ cup maple syrup
4 tbsp whiskey or bourbon
pinch of freshly grated nutmeg

54

Peach & Amaretto Crepes

1. Sift the flour and salt into a bowl. Add the milk, peach nectar, egg, and butter and beat to a smooth, bubbly batter. Let stand for 15 minutes.

2. Lightly grease an 8-inch/20-cm skillet and heat over medium heat. Pour in enough batter to just cover the skillet, swirling to cover in a fairly thin, even layer. Cook until the underside is golden, then flip or turn with a spatula or palette knife and cook the other side until golden brown.

3. Repeat this process, using the remaining batter. Interleave the cooked crepes with paper towels and keep warm.

4. For the filling, melt the butter in a wide saucepan over fairly high heat and add the peaches. Sprinkle with the sugar and cook for 2–3 minutes, stirring, until golden. Add the amaretto and remove from the heat.

5. Divide the peaches among the crepes and fold over. Spoon over the peach juices, sprinkle with the crushed amaretti cookies, and serve immediately.

Serves 4

- 1¼ cups all-purpose white flour
- pinch of salt
- 1 cup milk
- scant ½ cup peach nectar or orange juice
- 1 extra-large egg
- 2 tbsp melted butter
- butter, for greasing
- 12 amaretti cookies, crumbled, to serve

Filling
3 tbsp butter
2 ripe peaches, sliced
¼ cup superfine sugar
4 tbsp amaretto

Raspberry Waffle Sundae

1. Sift the flour, baking powder, salt, and sugar into a bowl. Add the milk, egg, butter, and vanilla extract and beat to a smooth batter. Let stand for 5 minutes.

2. Lightly grease a waffle maker and heat until hot. Pour the batter into the waffle maker and cook until golden brown. Repeat this process, using the remaining batter. Cut the waffles into wedges or triangles.

3. For the raspberry puree, place half of the raspberries in a blender with the lemon juice and confectioners' sugar and process until smooth.

4. Place scoops of ice cream in large sundae glasses with half of the remaining whole raspberries. Put 3–4 wedges of waffle in each glass, add a swirl of cream, and top with the remaining whole raspberries.

5. Spoon over the raspberry puree and serve immediately.

Serves 4–6

* 1¼ cups all-purpose white flour
* 1½ tsp baking powder
* pinch of salt
1 tbsp superfine sugar
* 1 cup milk
* 1 extra-large egg
* 2 tbsp melted butter
1 tsp vanilla extract
sunflower oil, for greasing
raspberry ripple ice cream and
    whipped cream, to serve

Raspberry puree
3¼ cups raspberries
1 tbsp lemon juice
1 tbsp confectioners' sugar

56

Blue Cheese & Basil Pancakes

1. Sift the flour, baking powder, and salt into a bowl. Add the milk, egg, egg yolks, cheese, and butter and beat to a smooth batter. Let stand for 5 minutes.

2. For the basil butter, place all the ingredients in a food processor or blender and process until smooth.

3. Lightly grease a griddle pan or skillet and heat over medium heat. Spoon tablespoons of batter into the pan and cook until bubbles appear on the surface.

4. Turn over with a spatula palette knife and cook the other side until golden brown. Repeat this process, using the remaining batter, while keeping the cooked pancakes warm.

5. Top the pancakes with the basil butter and serve immediately.

Serves 4

* 1¼ cups all-purpose white flour
* 1½ tsp baking powder
* pinch of salt
* 1 cup milk
* 1 extra-large egg
  2 egg yolks
  3½ oz/100 g blue cheese, mashed
* 2 tbsp melted butter
  sunflower oil, for greasing

Basil butter
large handful of fresh basil
⅔ cup butter, softened
juice of ½ lemon
1 garlic clove, crushed

57

Beer Waffles with Ham & Cheese

① Sift the flour, baking powder, salt, and dry mustard into a bowl. Add the beer, egg, and oil and beat to a smooth batter. Let stand for 5 minutes.

② Lightly grease a waffle maker and heat until hot. Pour the batter into the waffle maker and cook until golden brown. Repeat, using the remaining batter, while keeping the cooked waffles warm.

③ Preheat the broiler to high. Place the waffles on a baking sheet and arrange the ham on top. Sprinkle with grated cheese and broil until melted. Serve immediately.

Serves 4

* 1¼ cups all-purpose white flour
* 1½ tsp baking powder
* pinch of salt
  2 tsp dry English mustard
* 1 cup beer or lager
* 1 extra-large egg
* 2 tbsp sunflower oil, plus extra for greasing

Topping
8 thin slices smoked ham

1¼ cups coarsely grated Gruyère cheese or cheddar cheese

58

Shrimp & Garlic Butter Pancakes

1. Sift the flour, baking powder, and salt into a bowl. Add the milk, egg, and butter and beat to a smooth batter. Let stand for 5 minutes.

2. Lightly grease a griddle pan or skillet and heat over medium heat. Spoon tablespoons of batter into the pan and cook until bubbles appear on the surface.

3. Turn over with a spatula or palette knife and cook the other side until golden brown. Repeat this process, using the remaining batter, while keeping the cooked pancakes warm.

4. For the shrimp-and-garlic butter, heat the butter in a medium saucepan until melted, add the garlic and shrimp, and stir for 2–3 minutes, until the shrimp turn evenly pink. Add the lemon juice and parsley and season to taste with salt and pepper.

5. Spoon over the shrimp-and-garlic butter and serve immediately.

Serves 4

- 1¼ cups all-purpose white flour
- 1½ tsp baking powder
- pinch of salt
- 1 cup milk
- 1 large egg
- 2 tbsp melted butter
- sunflower oil, for greasing

Shrimp & garlic butter
- 7 tbsp butter
- 2 garlic cloves, crushed
- 14 oz/400 g peeled jumbo shrimp
- 1 tbsp lemon juice
- 2 tbsp chopped parsley
- salt and pepper

59

Fried Waffle Sandwich

1. Sift the flour, baking powder, and salt into a bowl. Add the milk, egg, and butter and beat to a smooth batter. Let stand for 5 minutes.

2. Lightly grease a waffle maker and heat until hot. Pour the batter into the waffle maker and cook until golden brown. Repeat, using the remaining batter, while keeping the cooked waffles warm.

3. Slice or break up the mozzarella and divide among half of the waffles. Top with basil leaves and season to taste with salt and pepper. Place another waffle on top of each.

4. Heat a shallow depth of oil in a skillet over high heat until very hot. Quickly dip the waffle sandwiches into the beaten egg, coating on both sides, then lower carefully into the oil and fry for about 30 seconds on each side, until golden and crisp.

5. Drain the waffles on paper towels and serve immediately.

Serves 4

* 1¼ cups all-purpose white flour
* 1½ tsp baking powder
* pinch of salt
* 1 cup milk
* 1 extra-large egg
* 2 tbsp melted butter
  olive oil, for greasing and frying

To serve
7 oz/200 g mozzarella cheese
1 cup fresh basil leaves
2 eggs, beaten
salt and pepper

60

Smoked Salmon & Mascarpone Rolls

1. Sift the flour and salt into a bowl. Add the milk, water, egg, and butter and beat to a smooth, bubbly batter. Stir in the dill and let stand for 15 minutes.

2. Lightly grease an 8-inch/20-cm skillet and heat over medium heat. Pour in enough batter to just cover the skillet, swirling to cover in a fairly thin, even layer. Cook until the underside is golden, then flip or turn with a spatula or palette knife and cook the other side until golden brown.

3. Repeat this process, using the remaining batter. Interleave the cooked crepes with paper towels.

4. Mix the mascarpone cheese with a little milk to soften, then spread some over each crepe. Arrange the smoked salmon over the mascarpone cheese and season to taste with pepper.

5. Firmly roll up the crepes to enclose the filling, cut into slices, and serve cold, sprinkled with dill.

Serves 4–6

* 1¼ cups all-purpose white flour
* pinch of salt
* 1 cup milk
  scant ½ cup water
* 1 extra-large egg
* 2 tbsp melted butter
  2 tbsp chopped fresh dill
  sunflower oil, for greasing

Filling
9 oz/250 g mascarpone cheese
1–2 tbsp milk
8 oz/225 g thinly sliced
  smoked salmon
pepper
dill sprigs, to garnish

Healthy

61

Cottage Cheese Pancakes

1. Sift the two types of flour, baking powder, salt, and sugar into a bowl, tipping in any bran left in the sifter. Add the cottage cheese, milk, egg, and oil and beat to a fairly thick batter. Let stand for 5 minutes.

2. Lightly grease a griddle pan or skillet and heat over medium heat. Spoon tablespoons of batter into the pan and cook until bubbles appear on the surface.

3. Turn over with a spatula or palette knife and cook the other side until golden brown. Repeat this process, using the remaining batter, while keeping the cooked pancakes warm.

4. Drizzle the pancakes with honey and serve immediately.

Serves 4

⅔ cup all-purpose white flour

⅔ cup whole wheat flour

1½ tsp baking powder

pinch of salt

1 tbsp dark brown sugar

generous 1 cup low-fat cottage cheese

½ cup skim milk

1 extra-large egg

2 tbsp sunflower oil, plus extra for greasing

clear honey, to serve

62

Dairy-Free
Pancakes with Orange

1. Sift the flour, baking powder, and salt into a bowl. Add the milk, egg, oil, and orange rind and beat to a smooth batter. Let stand for 5 minutes.

2. For the topping, cut away all the peel and white pith from the oranges and carefully remove the segments, catching the juices in a bowl. Mix the juices with the maple syrup.

3. Lightly grease a griddle pan or skillet and heat over medium heat. Spoon tablespoons of batter into the pan and cook until bubbles appear on the surface.

4. Turn over with a spatula or palette knife and cook the other side until golden brown. Repeat this process, using the remaining batter, while keeping the cooked pancakes warm.

5. Serve the pancakes warm with the orange segments, and the syrupy juices spooned over the top.

Serves 4

1⅓ cups white spelt flour
* 1½ tsp baking powder
* pinch of salt
* generous 1 cup sweetened soy milk
* 1 extra-large egg
* 2 tbsp sunflower oil, plus extra for greasing
  finely grated rind 1 orange

Topping
2 large oranges
3 tbsp maple syrup

63

Yogurt Waffles with Poached Apricots

1. For the topping, place the apricots in a saucepan with the apple juice and honey. Bring to a boil, stirring, then reduce the heat to low and cook gently for 10–15 minutes, or until tender.

2. Meanwhile, sift the two types of flour, baking powder, and salt into a bowl, adding back any bran from the sifter. Add the yogurt, egg, and oil and beat to a smooth batter. Let stand for 5 minutes.

3. Lightly grease a waffle maker and heat until hot. Pour the batter into the waffle maker and cook until golden brown. Repeat this process, using the remaining batter, while keeping the cooked waffles warm.

4. Spoon over the apricots and juices and serve immediately.

Serves 4

⅔ cup all-purpose white flour
⅔ cup whole-wheat flour
※ 1½ tsp baking powder
※ pinch of salt
※ 1 cup low-fat plain yogurt
※ 1 extra-large egg
※ 2 tbsp sunflower oil, plus extra for greasing

Topping
14 oz/400 g fresh apricots, pitted and halved
4 tbsp apple juice
1 tbsp honey

64

Poppy Seed & Lemon Crepes

1. Sift the flour and salt into a bowl. Add the milk, water, egg, and oil and beat to a smooth batter. Stir in the poppy seeds and lemon rind. Let stand for 15 minutes.

2. Lightly grease an 8-inch/20-cm skillet and heat over medium heat. Pour in enough batter to just cover the skillet, swirling to cover in a thin, even layer. Cook until the underside is golden, then flip or turn with a spatula or palette knife and cook the other side until golden brown.

3. Repeat this process, using the remaining batter. Interleave the cooked crepes with paper towels and keep warm.

4. Roll up or fold the crepes, sprinkle with honey and lemon juice, and serve immediately with extra poppy seeds sprinkled over the top.

Serves 4

* 1¼ cups all-purpose white flour
* pinch of salt
* 1 cup skim milk
  scant ½ cup water
* 1 extra-large egg
* 2 tbsp sunflower oil, plus extra for greasing
  1 tbsp poppy seeds, plus extra to serve
  finely grated rind and juice of 2 lemons
  honey, to serve

65

Oatmeal & Raisin Buttermilk Waffles

1. Sift the flour, baking powder, salt, and sugar into a bowl. Add the buttermilk, egg, oil, and water and beat to a smooth batter. Stir in the oats and raisins and let stand for 5 minutes.

2. Lightly grease a waffle maker and heat until hot. Pour the batter into the waffle maker and cook until golden brown. Repeat this process, using the remaining batter, while keeping the cooked waffles warm.

3. Serve immediately with maple syrup.

Serves 4

* 1¼ cups all-purpose white flour
* 1½ tsp baking powder
* pinch of salt
  1 tbsp dark brown sugar
* 1 cup buttermilk
* 1 extra-large egg
* 2 tbsp sunflower oil, plus extra for greasing
  2 tbsp water
  ⅔ cup quick-cooking rolled oats
  ½ cup raisins
  maple syrup or fruit preserves, to serve

66

Vanilla Waffles with Fruit Salsa

1. For the salsa, peel the kiwis and cut into ½-inch/1-cm dice. Place half of the strawberries in a food processor with the lemon juice and process to a smooth puree. Cut the remaining strawberries into ½-inch/1-cm dice and mix with the puree and kiwis.

2. Sift the flour, baking powder, salt, and sugar into a bowl. Add the milk, egg yolk, oil, and vanilla seeds and beat to a smooth batter. Whisk the egg white until soft peaks form, then fold into the batter.

3. Lightly grease a waffle maker and heat until hot. Pour the batter into the waffle maker and cook until golden brown. Repeat, using the remaining batter, while keeping the cooked waffles warm.

4. Spoon the fruit salsa over the waffles and serve warm.

Serves 4

* 1¼ cups all-purpose white flour
* 1½ tsp baking powder
* pinch of salt
  1 tbsp confectioners' sugar
* 1 cup skim milk
* 1 extra-large egg, separated
* 2 tbsp sunflower oil, plus extra for greasing
  seeds from 1 vanilla bean

Salsa
2 kiwis
8 oz/225 g strawberries
1 tbsp lemon juice

67

Peach-Filled Cranberry Crepes

1. Sift the flour and salt into a bowl. Add the milk, cranberry juice, egg, and oil and beat to a smooth, bubbly batter. Let stand for 15 minutes.

2. Meanwhile, for the filling, halve, pit, and chop the peaches. Place in a medium saucepan with the cranberry juice and heat over medium heat until boiling, then remove from the heat and keep warm.

3. Lightly grease an 8-inch/20-cm skillet and heat over medium heat. Pour in enough batter to just cover the skillet, swirling to cover in a thin, even layer. Cook until the underside is golden, then flip or turn with a spatula or palette knife and cook the other side until golden brown.

4. Repeat this process, using the remaining batter. Interleave the cooked crepes with paper towels and keep warm.

5. Divide the peaches among the crepes and top each crepe with a spoonful of yogurt. Fold over into fan shapes and serve immediately, with the peach juices spooned over.

Serves 4

- 1¼ cups all-purpose white flour
- pinch of salt
- 1 cup lowfat milk
  scant ½ cup cranberry juice
- 1 extra-large egg
- 2 tbsp sunflower oil, plus extra for greasing

Filling
4 ripe peaches or nectarines
3 tbsp cranberry juice
⅔ cup plain low-fat yogurt

68

Low-Fat Apple Waffles

1. Sift the flour, baking powder, salt, and sugar into a bowl. Add the milk, oil, and 1 egg white and beat to a smooth batter. Stir in the grated apples and orange rind. Whisk the remaining egg white until soft peaks form, then fold into the batter.

2. Thoroughly grease a waffle maker and heat until hot. Pour the batter into the waffle maker and cook until golden brown. Repeat, using the remaining batter, while keeping the cooked waffles warm.

3. Meanwhile, core and slice the red apples and sprinkle with orange juice. Top the waffles with the apple slices and serve immediately.

Serves 4

- 1¼ cups all-purpose white flour
- 1½ tsp baking powder
- pinch of salt
- 1 tbsp superfine sugar
- 1 cup skim milk
- 1 tbsp sunflower oil, plus extra for greasing
- 2 extra-large egg whites
- 2 small crisp apples, cored and grated
- finely grated rind of 1 small orange
- 2 red apples and some orange juice, to serve

69

Multigrain Pancakes

1. Sift the two types of flour, baking powder, and salt into a bowl, tipping in any bran left in the sifter. Add the buttermilk, egg, oil, and honey and beat to a smooth batter. Stir in the oats and seeds and let stand for 5 minutes.

2. Lightly grease a griddle pan or skillet and heat over medium heat. Spoon tablespoons of batter into the pan and cook until bubbles appear on the surface.

3. Turn over with a spatula or palette knife and cook the other side until golden brown. Repeat this process, using the remaining batter, while keeping the cooked pancakes warm.

4. Pour the agave syrup over the pancakes, sprinkle with pumpkin seeds and serve immediately.

Serves 4

⅔ cup all-purpose white flour

⅔ cup whole wheat flour

✳ 1½ tsp baking powder

✳ pinch of salt

✳ 1 cup buttermilk

✳ 1 extra-large egg

✳ 2 tbsp sunflower oil, plus extra for greasing

1 tbsp honey

scant ½ cup rolled oats

2 tbsp sunflower seeds

2 tbsp pumpkin seeds, plus extra to decorate

1 tbsp sesame seeds

agave syrup or maple syrup, to serve

70

Beet Waffles

1. Sift the flour, baking powder, and salt into a bowl. Add the milk, egg, and oil and beat to a smooth batter. Stir in the beet, thyme, and horseradish sauce and let stand for 5 minutes.

2. Lightly grease a waffle maker and heat until hot. Pour the batter into the waffle maker and cook until golden brown. Repeat this process, using the remaining batter, while keeping the cooked waffles warm.

3. Serve immediately, with a spoonful of yogurt.

Serves 4

* 1¼ cups all-purpose white flour
* 1½ tsp baking powder
* pinch of salt
* 1 cup lowfat milk
* 1 extra-large egg
* 2 tbsp sunflower oil, plus extra for greasing
* scant 1½ cups grated fresh beet
* 1 tsp dried thyme
* 1 tbsp horseradish sauce
* Greek-style yogurt or fromage frais, to serve

71

Spinach Crepe Pockets

1. Sift the two types of flour and the salt into a bowl, tipping in any bran left in the sifter. Add the milk, water, egg, oil, and spinach and beat to a smooth, bubbly batter. Let stand for 15 minutes.

2. Lightly grease an 8-inch/20-cm skillet and heat over medium heat. Pour in enough batter to just cover the skillet, swirling to cover evenly. Cook until the underside is golden, then flip or turn with a spatula or palette knife and cook the other side until golden brown.

3. Use the remaining batter to make 8 crepes. Interleave the cooked crepes with paper towels and keep warm. Preheat the oven to 425°F/220°C.

4. For the filling, place the vegetable oil spread, flour, and milk in a saucepan over medium heat and, using a handheld mixer, beat until boiling. Cook for an additional 2 minutes, stirring, until thickened and smooth.

5. Stir in the tuna, corn kernels, onion, and salt and pepper to taste. Spoon a little of the filling into the center of each crepe and fold over the sides to make a bundle.

6. Place the bundles in an ovenproof dish, with the seams underneath. Brush lightly with oil and bake in the preheated oven for about 10 minutes, until bubbling. Serve immediately.

Serves 8

⅔ cup all-purpose white flour

⅔ cup whole wheat flour

✳ pinch of salt

✳ 1 cup skim milk

4 tbsp water

✳ 1 extra-large egg

✳ 2 tbsp olive oil, plus extra for brushing and greasing

⅓ cup finely chopped, cooked spinach

Filling

2 tbsp vegetable oil spread, margarine, or butter

3 tbsp all-purpose white flour

1 cup skim milk

13 oz/375 g canned tuna, drained and flaked

11¾ oz/340 g canned corn kernels, drained

1 small red onion, grated

salt and pepper

Tomato Pancake Stack

1. Sift the two types of flour, baking powder, and salt into a bowl, tipping in any bran left in the sifter. Add the tomato juice, tomato paste, egg, oil, and pepper and beat to a smooth batter. Let stand for 5 minutes.

2. Lightly grease a griddle pan or skillet and heat over medium heat. Spoon tablespoons of batter into the pan and cook until bubbles appear on the surface.

3. Turn over with a spatula or palette knife and cook the other side until golden brown. Repeat this process, using the remaining batter, while keeping the cooked pancakes warm.

4. Slice the tomatoes and stack them with the pancakes, interleaved with basil leaves. Top with a spoonful of yogurt and sprinkle with paprika.

Serves 4

⅔ cup all-purpose white flour
⅔ cup whole wheat flour
✳ 1½ tsp baking powder
✳ pinch of salt
✳ 1 cup tomato juice
1 tbsp tomato paste
✳ 1 extra-large egg
✳ 2 tbsp olive oil
½ tsp pepper
sunflower oil, for greasing

Filling
3 beef tomatoes
12–16 fresh basil leaves
⅔ cup low-fat plain yogurt
paprika, for dusting

Vegetarian Waffles

1. Sift the two types of flour, baking powder, and salt into a bowl, tipping in any bran left in the sifter. Add the milk, egg, and oil and beat to a smooth batter. Stir in the cilantro and let stand for 5 minutes.

2. Lightly grease a waffle maker and heat until hot. Pour the batter into the waffle maker and cook until golden brown. Repeat, using the remaining batter, while keeping the cooked waffles warm.

3. For the topping, heat the peanut oil and sesame oil in a wok over high heat, then add the tofu and gently stir-fry until golden brown. Remove and keep hot. Add the onion, ginger, garlic, and broccoli to the wok and stir-fry for 3–4 minutes, until tender. Stir in the tamari, then spoon over the waffles.

4. Serve immediately with extra tamari.

Serves 4

⅔ cup all-purpose white flour

⅔ cup whole wheat flour

1½ tsp baking powder

pinch of salt

1 cup soy milk

1 extra-large egg

2 tbsp peanut oil, plus extra for greasing

3 tbsp chopped cilantro

Topping

2 tbsp peanut oil

1 tbsp sesame oil

12 oz/350 g firm tofu, cut into ½-inch/1-cm cubes

1 onion, thinly sliced

1 tbsp finely chopped fresh ginger

1 garlic clove, thinly sliced

3½ cups small broccoli florets

1 tbsp tamari or soy sauce, plus extra to serve

74

Wild Rice Pancakes with Guacamole

1. Sift the flour, baking powder, and salt into a bowl. Add the milk, egg, and oil and beat to a smooth batter. Stir in the rice and let stand for 5 minutes.

2. For the guacamole, halve and pit the avocados and scoop out the flesh. Mash with a fork and stir in the lime juice, garlic, tomatoes, and chile. Season to taste with salt and pepper.

3. Lightly grease a griddle pan or skillet and heat over medium heat. Spoon tablespoons of the batter into the pan and cook until bubbles appear on the surface.

4. Turn or flip over with a spatula or palette knife and cook the other side until golden brown. Repeat this process, using the remaining batter, while keeping the cooked pancakes warm.

5. Serve immediately with the guacamole.

Serves 4

* 1¼ cups all-purpose white flour
* 1½ tsp baking powder
* pinch of salt
* 1 cup skim milk
* 1 extra-large egg
* 2 tbsp sunflower oil, plus extra for greasing
  1 cup cooked wild rice

Guacamole
2 ripe avocados
2 tbsp lime juice
1 garlic clove, crushed
2 tomatoes, chopped
1 small red chile, finely chopped
salt and pepper

Buckwheat Crepes

1. Sift the flour and salt into a bowl. Add the milk, water, egg, and oil and beat to a smooth, bubbly batter. Let stand for 15 minutes.

2. Lightly grease an 8-inch/20-cm skillet and heat over medium heat. Pour in enough batter to just cover the skillet, swirling to cover in a fairly thin, even layer. Cook until the underside is golden, then flip or turn with a spatula or palette knife and cook the other side until golden brown.

3. Repeat this process, using the remaining batter. Interleave the cooked crepes with paper towels and keep warm.

4. For the filling, heat the oil in a skillet over medium heat, add the shallots, and fry, stirring frequently, until softened. Add the nuts and stir until golden, then remove from the heat and add the parsley, and salt and pepper to taste.

5. Roll up or fold the crepes, spoon over the cashew nut mixture, and serve immediately.

Serves 4

* 1¼ cups buckwheat flour
* pinch of salt
* generous 1 cup lowfat milk
  scant ½ cup water
* 1 extra-large egg
* 2 tbsp olive oil
  sunflower oil, for greasing

Filling
2 tbsp olive oil
2 shallots, finely chopped
1⅓ cups cashew nuts
2 tbsp chopped parsley
salt and pepper

Spiced Crepes with Watermelon & Feta

1. Sift the flour, salt, and spices into a bowl. Add the milk, water, egg, and butter and beat to a smooth, bubbly batter. Let stand for 15 minutes.

2. Lightly grease an 8-inch/20-cm skillet and heat over medium heat. Pour in enough batter to just cover the skillet, swirling to cover in a fairly thin, even layer. Cook until the underside is golden, then flip or turn with a spatula or palette knife and cook the other side until golden brown.

3. Repeat this process, using the remaining batter. Interleave the cooked crepes with paper towels and keep warm.

4. Divide the watercress, watermelon, and cheese between the crepes, sprinkle with mint, fold over, and serve immediately.

Serves 4

1⅔ cups chickpea flour

pinch of salt

½ tsp turmeric

½ tsp chili powder

1 cup skim milk

scant ½ cup water

1 extra-large egg

2 tbsp melted butter

sunflower oil, for greasing

Filling

1 bunch watercress

½ small watermelon, cut in quarters lengthwise and sliced

1⅓ cups crumbled feta cheese

chopped mint, for sprinkling

77

Sun-Dried Tomato & Olive Waffles

1. Sift the flour, baking powder, and salt into a bowl. Add the milk, egg, and oil and beat to a smooth batter. Stir in the tomatoes and olives and let stand for 5 minutes.

2. Lightly grease a waffle maker and heat until hot. Pour the batter into the waffle maker and cook until golden brown. Repeat this process, using the remaining batter, while keeping the cooked waffles warm.

3. Drizzle over some balsamic glaze and serve immediately.

Serves 4

* 1¼ cups all-purpose white flour
* 1½ tsp baking powder
* pinch of salt
* 1 cup lowfat milk
* 1 extra-large egg
* 2 tbsp olive oil
* ½ cup drained and finely chopped sun-dried tomatoes in oil
* 12 black olives, pitted and finely chopped
* sunflower oil, for greasing
* balsamic glaze, to serve

78

Chili Bean Crepes

1. Sift the two types of flour and the salt into a bowl, tipping in any bran left in the sifter. Add the milk, tomato juice, egg, and oil and beat to a smooth, bubbly batter. Stir in the parsley and let stand for 15 minutes.

2. For the filling, place the kidney beans and cannellini beans in a large saucepan over medium heat and add the crushed pepper, garlic, and tomatoes. Heat gently until boiling, then reduce the heat, season to taste with salt and pepper, and keep warm.

3. Lightly grease an 8-inch/20-cm skillet and heat over medium heat. Pour in enough batter to just cover the skillet, swirling to cover in a thin, even layer. Cook until the underside is golden, then flip or turn with a spatula or palette knife and cook the other side until golden brown.

4. Repeat this process, using the remaining batter. Interleave the cooked crepes with paper towels and keep warm.

5. Divide the bean mixture among the crepes, then roll or fold them over and serve immediately.

Serves 4

⅔ cup all-purpose white flour

⅔ cup whole wheat flour

✳ pinch of salt

✳ 1 cup lowfat milk

scant ½ cup juice from the canned tomatoes used in the filling (made up with water, if necessary)

✳ 1 extra-large egg

✳ 2 tbsp olive oil

2 tbsp finely chopped parsley

sunflower oil, for greasing

Filling

14 oz/400 g canned red kidney beans, drained

14 oz/400 g canned cannellini beans, drained

½ tsp crushed red pepper

1 garlic clove, crushed

14 oz/400 g canned chopped tomatoes, drained, juice reserved for the crepe batter

salt and pepper

Waffle Hummus Sandwich

1. For the salsa, mix together the tomatoes, chile, onion, cilantro, lemon juice, and oil. Season to taste with salt and pepper and let stand for about 30 minutes.

2. Sift the two types of flour, baking powder, and salt into a bowl, tipping in any bran left in the sifter. Add the milk, egg, and oil and beat to a smooth batter. Let stand for 5 minutes.

3. Lightly grease a waffle maker and heat until hot. Pour the batter into the waffle maker and cook until golden brown. Repeat this process, using the remaining batter, while keeping the cooked waffles warm.

4. Spread the waffles with hummus, then sandwich together in pairs with arugula leaves and a spoonful of salsa.

5. Serve immediately, with the remaining salsa.

Serves 4

⅔ cup all-purpose white flour
⅔ cup whole wheat flour
1½ tsp baking powder
pinch of salt
1 cup lowfat milk
1 extra-large egg
2 tbsp sunflower oil, plus extra for greasing
¾ cup hummus and a handful of arugula leaves, to serve

Salsa
3 ripe tomatoes, finely diced
1 small red chile, finely chopped
1 small red onion, finely diced
2 tbsp chopped cilantro
juice of ½ lemon
1 tbsp olive oil
salt and pepper

Zucchini Pancakes

1. Sift the two types of flour, baking powder, and salt into a bowl, tipping in any bran left in the sifter. Add the milk, egg, and oil and beat to a smooth batter. Stir in the grated zucchini and oregano and let stand for 5 minutes.

2. For the salsa, stir together the bell pepper, tomato, lime, honey, and oil. Season to taste with salt and pepper.

3. Lightly grease a griddle pan or skillet and heat over medium heat. Spoon tablespoons of batter into the pan and cook until bubbles appear on the surface.

4. Turn over with a spatula or palette knife and cook the other side until golden brown. Repeat this process, using the remaining batter, while keeping the cooked pancakes warm.

5. Serve immediately, with a spoonful of salsa.

Serves 4

⅔ cup all-purpose white flour
⅔ cup whole wheat flour
1½ tsp baking powder
pinch of salt
1 cup lowfat milk
1 extra-large egg
2 tbsp sunflower oil, plus extra for greasing
2 small zucchini, grated
1 tsp dried oregano

Salsa
1 red bell pepper, seeded and finely diced
1 large tomato, finely diced
juice of ½ lime
1 tsp honey
2 tbsp extra virgin olive oil
salt and pepper

Special Occasion

Thai Coconut Crepes

1 Sift the flour, sugar, and salt into a bowl. Add the coconut milk, water, egg, and oil and beat to a smooth batter. Add a little food coloring, if using, to tint the batter to a delicate pale green. Let stand for 15 minutes.

2 Lightly grease an 8-inch/20-cm skillet and heat over medium heat. Pour in enough batter to just cover the skillet, swirling to cover in a thin, even layer. Cook until the underside is golden, then flip or turn with a spatula or palette knife and cook the other side until golden brown.

3 Repeat this process, using the remaining batter. Interleave the cooked crepes with paper towels and keep warm.

4 Sprinkle the crepes with grated coconut and jaggery, fold into fan shapes, then sprinkle with lime juice and serve immediately.

Serves 4

※ 1 cup rice flour
2 tbsp superfine sugar
※ pinch of salt
※ 1 cup coconut milk
scant ½ cup water
※ 1 extra-large egg
※ 2 tbsp sunflower oil, plus extra for greasing
a few drops of green food coloring (optional)

To serve
1¼ cups freshly grated coconut or 1 cup dry unsweetened shredded coconut
2 tbsp crumbled jaggery
juice of 1 lime

Christmas Spiced Pancakes

1. Sift the flour, baking powder, salt, and allspice into a bowl. Add the milk, egg, and butter and beat to a smooth batter. Stir in the cranberries, mixed peel, and nuts and let stand for 5 minutes.

2. Lightly grease a griddle pan or skillet and heat over medium heat. Spoon tablespoons of batter into the pan to make oval shapes, and cook until bubbles appear on the surface.

3. Turn over with a palette knife and cook the other side until golden brown. Repeat this process, using the remaining batter, while keeping the cooked pancakes warm.

4. For the syrup, place the sugar and water in a small saucepan and heat over low heat, stirring, until the sugar dissolves. Bring to a boil and boil for 1 minute, then add the rum and vanilla and return to a boil. Remove from the heat.

5. Spoon the syrup over the pancakes and serve immediately.

Serves 4

- 1¼ cups all-purpose white flour
- 1½ tsp baking powder
- pinch of salt
- 1 tsp allspice
- 1 cup milk
- 1 extra-large egg
- 2 tbsp melted butter
- 1 cup chopped cranberries
- ¼ cup chopped mixed candied peel
- ¼ cup mixed chopped nuts
- sunflower oil, for greasing

Syrup
2 tbsp dark brown sugar
4 tbsp water
3 tbsp dark rum
1 tsp vanilla extract

Strawberry Sticks

1. Sift the flour, salt, and sugar into a bowl. Add the milk, water, egg, butter, and vanilla extract and beat to a smooth, bubbly batter. Let stand for 15 minutes.

2. Lightly grease an 8-inch/20-cm skillet and heat over medium heat. Pour in enough batter to just cover the skillet, swirling to cover in a thin, even layer. Cook until the underside is golden, then flip or turn with a spatula or palette knife and cook the other side until golden.

3. Repeat this process, using the remaining batter. Interleave the cooked crepes with paper towels and keep warm.

4. To serve, sprinkle the crepes with vanilla sugar, roll up firmly, and cut diagonally into 1-inch/2.5-cm-thick slices. Thread onto about 12 small bamboo skewers with the strawberries between, arrange on a platter, and serve immediately.

Serves 4–6

* 1¼ cups all-purpose white flour
* pinch of salt
  1 tbsp superfine sugar
* 1 cup milk
  scant ½ cup water
* 1 extra-large egg
* 2 tbsp melted butter
  1 tsp vanilla extract
  butter, for greasing
  vanilla sugar and fresh
    strawberries, to serve

Crêpes Suzettes

1. Sift the flour and salt into a bowl. Add the milk, water, egg, and butter and beat to a smooth, bubbly batter. Let stand for 15 minutes.

2. Melt ½ teaspoon of the butter in an 8-inch/20-cm skillet over medium heat. Pour in enough batter to just cover the skillet, swirling to cover in a thin, even layer. Cook until the underside is golden, then flip or turn with a spatula or palette knife and cook the other side until golden brown.

3. Repeat this process, using the remaining batter. Interleave the cooked crepes with paper towels and keep warm.

4. For the sauce, place the butter and sugar in a wide skillet over medium heat and stir until melted. Stir in the orange rind and juice with 2 tablespoons of the liqueur and bring to a boil.

5. Fold the crepes into quarters and add to the skillet, spooning over the sauce until evenly heated.

6. To serve, heat the remaining liqueur in a ladle, pour over the crepes, and set alight. Serve immediately, sprinkled with orange zest.

Serves 4

* 1¼ cups all-purpose white flour
* pinch of salt
* 1 cup milk
  scant ½ cup water
* 1 extra-large egg
* 2 tbsp melted butter
  butter, for frying
  shreds of orange zest, to decorate

Sauce
7 tbsp butter
½ cup superfine sugar
finely grated rind and juice of 1 orange
scant ½ cup orange liqueur, such as Grand Marnier or Cointreau

85

Valentine Waffles

1. For the sauce, melt the chocolate with the cream and rum in a bowl over a saucepan of barely simmering water. Stir until smooth, remove from the heat, and keep warm.

2. Sift the flour, baking powder, and salt into a bowl. Add the milk, egg, and oil and beat to a smooth batter. Let stand for 5 minutes.

3. Lightly grease a waffle maker and heat until hot. Pour the batter into the waffle maker and cook until golden brown. Repeat, using the remaining batter, while keeping the cooked waffles warm.

4. Using a heart-shaped cutter approximately 2¾ inches/7 cm in diameter, stamp a heart shape from the center of each waffle.

5. Serve the waffles on individual plates, with the raspberries in the center, the chocolate sauce poured around, and the heart-shaped cutouts on the side.

Serves 4

* 1¼ cups all-purpose white flour
* 1½ tsp baking powder
* pinch of salt
* 1 cup milk
* 1 extra-large egg
* 2 tbsp sunflower oil, plus extra for greasing
  1⅔ cups raspberries, to serve

Chocolate sauce
3½ oz/100 g semisweet dark chocolate
4 tbsp light cream
1 tbsp dark rum or brandy

86

Pancakes Soufflé

1. For the syrup, place the strawberries in a food processor with the confectioners' sugar and rum. Process until smooth and rub through a strainer to remove any seeds.

2. Sift the flour, baking powder, salt, and sugar into a bowl. Add the milk, egg yolk, butter, and 1 teaspoon of the vanilla extract and beat to a smooth batter. Whisk the egg whites until soft peaks form, then fold into the batter.

3. Lightly grease a griddle pan or skillet and heat over medium heat. Spoon tablespoons of batter into the pan and cook the pancakes until they puff up.

4. Turn over with a spatula or palette knife and cook the other side until golden brown. Repeat this process, using the remaining batter, while keeping the cooked pancakes warm (the pancakes will sink, but remain very light.)

5. Whip the cream with the confectioners' sugar and the remaining vanilla extract until it just holds soft peaks. Arrange the pancakes in stacks, spoon the cream on top, drizzle over the strawberry syrup, and serve immediately.

Serves 6

* 1¼ cups all-purpose white flour
* 1½ tsp baking powder
* pinch of salt
  2 tbsp superfine sugar
* 1 cup milk
* 1 extra-large egg, separated
* 2 tbsp melted butter
  2 tsp vanilla extract
  2 extra-large egg whites
  oil, for greasing
  generous 1 cup heavy cream and 1 tbsp confectioners' sugar, to serve

Strawberry syrup
9 oz/250 g strawberries
1 tbsp confectioners' sugar
1 tbsp white rum

87

Mixed Berry Pancake Stack

1. Sift the flour, baking powder, salt, and sugar into a bowl. Add the milk, egg, butter, and mint and beat to a smooth batter. Let stand for 5 minutes.

2. Lightly grease a griddle pan or skillet and heat over medium heat. Spoon tablespoons of batter into the pan and cook until bubbles appear on the surface.

3. Turn over with a spatula or palette knife and cook the other side until golden brown. Repeat this process, using the remaining batter, while keeping the cooked pancakes warm.

4. To serve, stack the pancakes with the yogurt and berries, decorate with mint sprigs, dust with confectioners' sugar, and serve immediately.

Serves 4

- 1¼ cups all-purpose white flour
- 1½ tsp baking powder
- pinch of salt
- 1 tbsp superfine sugar
- 1 cup milk
- 1 extra-large egg
- 2 tbsp melted butter
- 2 tbsp finely chopped fresh mint
- sunflower oil, for greasing

To serve
- scant 1 cup Greek-style plain yogurt
- 2½–2¾ cups mixed berries, such as blackberries, raspberries, red currants, and blueberries
- confectioners' sugar, for dusting
- fresh mint sprigs, to decorate

88

Pumpkin & Spice Pancakes

1. Sift the flour, baking powder, sugar, spices, and salt into a bowl. Add the milk, egg, and butter and beat to a smooth batter. Stir in the pumpkin and let stand for 5 minutes.

2. Lightly grease a griddle pan or skillet and heat over medium heat. Spoon tablespoons of batter into the pan and cook until bubbles appear on the surface.

3. Turn over with a spatula or palette knife and cook the other side until golden brown. Repeat this process, using the remaining batter, while keeping the cooked pancakes warm.

4. Mix the sugar and pumpkin pie spice together and sprinkle over the pancakes, then drizzle with melted butter and serve immediately.

Serves 4

- 1¼ cups all-purpose white flour
- 1½ tsp baking powder
- 2 tbsp dark brown sugar
- 1 tsp pumkin pie spice
- ½ tsp ground nutmeg
- pinch of salt
- 1 cup milk
- 1 extra-large egg
- 2 tbsp melted butter, plus extra to serve
- ¾ cup mashed cooked pumpkin
- sunflower oil, for greasing
- 2 tbsp raw brown sugar and ½ tsp pumpkin pie spice, to serve

89

Coconut Waffles with Mango

1. For the topping, place the ginger, syrup, and butter in a wide saucepan over medium heat pan and heat until the butter is melted. Add the mango slices and keep warm.

2. Sift the flour, baking powder, salt, and sugar into a bowl. Add the coconut milk, egg, and butter and beat to a smooth batter. Stir in the coconut and let stand for 5 minutes.

3. Lightly grease a waffle maker and heat until hot. Pour the batter into the waffle maker and cook until golden brown. Repeat, using the remaining batter, while keeping the cooked waffles warm.

4. Spoon over the ginger and mango syrup and serve immediately.

Serves 4

* 1¼ cups all-purpose white flour
* 1½ tsp baking powder
* pinch of salt
  1 tbsp superfine sugar
* 1 cup coconut milk
* 1 extra-large egg
* 2 tbsp melted butter
  2 tbsp dry unsweetened flaked coconut
  sunflower oil, for greasing

Topping
2 tbsp finely diced preserved ginger
3 tbsp preserved ginger syrup
3 tbsp butter
1 large mango, sliced

Cherry Crepe Baskets

1. Sift the flour and salt into a bowl. Add the milk, orange juice, egg, and butter and beat to a smooth, bubbly batter. Let stand for 15 minutes.

2. Lightly grease an 8-inch/20-cm skillet and heat over medium heat. Pour in enough batter to just cover the skillet, swirling to cover in a fairly thin, even layer. Cook until the underside is golden, then flip or turn with a spatula or palette knife and cook the other side until golden brown.

3. Repeat this process, using the remaining batter. Interleave the cooked crepes with paper towels and keep warm.

4. Preheat the oven to 400°F/200°C. Place 8–10 individual metal molds on a baking sheet, brush with oil, and drape the pancakes over. You can do this in batches.

5. Bake the crepes in the preheated oven for about 10 minutes, until set into shape. Remove carefully and place on serving plates. Mix the ricotta cheese, sugar, vanilla extract, and cherries together and spoon into the baskets.

6. Decorate with whole cherries and serve immediately.

Serves 4

- 1¼ cups all-purpose white flour
- pinch of salt
- 1 cup milk
- scant ½ cup orange juice
- 1 extra-large egg
- 2 tbsp melted butter
- sunflower oil, for greasing
- whole cherries, to decorate

Filling
- 1 cup ricotta cheese
- 2 tbsp confectioners' sugar
- 1 tsp vanilla extract
- 2½ cups pitted cherries

Children's Party Waffles

1. Sift the flour, baking powder, salt, and sugar into a bowl. Add the milk, egg, and butter and beat to a smooth batter.

2. Divide the batter between two separate pitchers and stir a few drops of pink or green food coloring into each. Let stand for 5 minutes.

3. Lightly grease a waffle maker and heat until hot. Pour the batters into separate compartments of the waffle maker and cook in batches until golden brown, while keeping the cooked waffles warm.

4. Decorate the waffles with the colored sprinkles and serve with the honey.

Serves 4–8

* 1¼ cups all-purpose white flour
* 1½ tsp baking powder
* pinch of salt
  1 tbsp superfine sugar
* 1 cup milk
* 1 extra-large egg
* 2 tbsp melted butter
  pink and green natural food colorings
  sunflower oil, for greasing
  colored sprinkles, to decorate
  honey, to serve

Red, White & Blue Pancakes

1. For the white chocolate sauce, place the cream and chocolate in a small saucepan over low heat and heat gently, stirring occasionally, until melted and smooth. Remove from the heat, stir in the vanilla extract, and keep warm.

2. Sift the flour, baking powder, salt, and sugar into a bowl. Add the milk, egg, and oil and beat to a smooth batter. Stir in the blueberries and cranberries and let stand for 5 minutes.

3. Lightly grease a griddle pan or skillet and heat over medium heat. Spoon tablespoons of batter into the pan and cook until bubbles appear on the surface.

4. Turn over with a spatula or palette knife and cook the other side until golden brown. Repeat this process, using the remaining batter, while keeping the cooked pancakes warm.

5. Spoon over the white chocolate sauce, sprinkle with the blueberries and cranberries, and serve immediately.

Serves 4

- 1¼ cups all-purpose white flour
- 1½ tsp baking powder
- pinch of salt
- 1 tbsp superfine sugar
- 1 cup milk
- 1 extra-large egg
- 2 tbsp sunflower oil, plus extra for greasing
- generous ¾ cup fresh blueberries, plus extra to serve
- scant ⅔ cup dried cranberries, plus extra to serve

White chocolate sauce
⅔ cup light cream
5½ oz/150 g white chocolate
1 tsp vanilla extract

93

Lacy Crepes with Sugared Rose Petals

1. For the sugared rose petals, use a small paintbrush to brush the rose petals with the egg white. Dust with the sugar and place on a sheet of nonstick parchment paper. Let stand in a dry place.

2. Sift the flour, salt, and sugar into a bowl. Add the milk, water, egg, butter, and rose water and beat to a smooth, bubbly batter. Pour into a squeeze sauce bottle and let stand for 15 minutes.

3. Lightly grease an 8-inch/20-cm skillet and heat over medium heat. Drizzle the batter all over the skillet to create a lacy effect in a fairly thin, even layer. Cook until just set, then flip or turn with a spatula or palette knife and cook the other side until golden brown.

4. Repeat this process, using the remaining batter. Interleave the cooked crepes with paper towels and keep warm.

5. Arrange the crepes loosely in fan shapes on serving plates, top with the sugared rose petals, and serve warm.

Serves 6

* 1¼ cups all-purpose white flour
* pinch of salt
  1 tbsp superfine sugar
* 1 cup milk
  scant ½ cup water
* 1 extra-large egg
* 2 tbsp melted butter
  1 tsp rose water
  sunflower oil, for greasing

Sugared rose petals
pink rose petals
1 egg white, lightly beaten
superfine sugar, for dusting

94

Pesto & Parmesan Canapés

1. Sift the flour, baking powder, and salt into a bowl. Add the milk, egg, oil, and pesto and beat to a smooth batter. Let stand for 5 minutes.

2. Lightly grease a griddle pan or skillet and heat over medium heat. Spoon teaspoons of batter into the pan and cook until bubbles appear on the surface.

3. Turn over with a spatula or palette knife and cook the other side until golden brown. Repeat this process, using the remaining batter, while keeping the cooked pancakes warm.

4. Place a small dollop of pesto on each pancake, top with cheese shavings, garnish with basil sprigs, and serve immediately.

Serves 10–12

* 1¼ cups all-purpose white flour
* 1½ tsp baking powder
* pinch of salt
* 1 cup milk
* 1 extra-large egg
* 2 tbsp sunflower oil, plus extra for greasing
* 3 tbsp red pesto or green pesto, plus extra to serve
* Parmesan cheese shavings, to serve
* fresh basil sprigs, to garnish

Turkey Salad Wraps

1. Sift the flour and salt into a bowl. Add the milk, water, egg, and butter and beat to a smooth, bubbly batter. Stir in the scallions and let stand for 15 minutes.

2. Lightly grease a 9-inch/23-cm skillet and heat over medium heat. Pour in enough batter to just cover the skillet, swirling to cover evenly. Cook until the underside is golden, then flip or turn with a spatula or palette knife and cook the other side until golden brown.

3. Repeat this process, using the remaining batter. Interleave the cooked crepes with paper towels and let cool.

4. For the filling, mix the mayonnaise and lemon juice together and season to taste with salt and pepper. Spread this mixture over one side of each crepe, then sprinkle with nuts and top with lettuce and slices of turkey.

5. Fold the other side of each crepe over the sides to form a wrap to hold the filling. Add a spoonful of cranberry sauce and serve cold.

Serves 6

* 1¼ cups all-purpose white flour
* pinch of salt
* 1 cup milk
  4 tbsp water
* 1 extra-large egg
* 2 tbsp melted butter
  4 scallions, very finely chopped
  sunflower oil, for greasing

Filling
4 tbsp mayonnaise
1 tbsp lemon juice
½ cup chopped pecans
½ small romaine lettuce, shredded
12 oz/350 g cooked turkey slices
4 tbsp cranberry sauce
salt and pepper

Salami Roll Ups

1. Place the water and herbs in a food processor and process until almost smooth. Sift the flour and salt into a bowl. Add the milk, egg, oil, and herb liquid and beat to a smooth, bubbly batter. Let stand for 15 minutes.

2. Lightly grease a 9-inch/23-cm skillet and heat over medium heat. Pour in enough batter to just cover the skillet, swirling to cover in a fairly thin, even layer. Cook until the underside is golden, then flip or turn with a spatula or palette knife and cook the other side until golden brown.

3. Repeat this process, using the remaining batter. Interleave the cooked crepes with paper towels and keep warm.

4. Mix together the mascarpone cheese and mayonnaise and spread over the crepes. Arrange the salami slices on top and roll up firmly.

5. Cut the rolls into ¾-inch/2-cm-thick slices and spear each with a toothpick to hold in place. Serve as canapés.

Serves 6–8

scant ½ cup water

3 tbsp chopped summer herbs, such as parsley, chives, and chervil

✳ 1¼ cups all-purpose white flour

✳ pinch of salt

✳ 1 cup milk

✳ 1 extra-large egg

✳ 2 tbsp olive oil

sunflower oil, for greasing

Filling
3½ oz/100 g mascarpone cheese

3 tbsp mayonnaise

8 oz/225 g salami Milano, thinly sliced

Asian Pancake Rolls

1. Sift the flour and salt into a bowl. Add the milk, water, egg, and oil and beat to a smooth, bubbly batter. Let stand for 15 minutes.

2. Lightly grease an 8-inch/20-cm skillet and heat over medium heat. Pour in enough batter to cover the skillet, swirling to cover in a fairly thin, even layer. Cook until the underside is golden, then flip or turn with a spatula or palette knife and cook the other side until golden brown.

3. Repeat this process, using the remaining batter. Interleave the cooked crepes with paper towels and keep warm.

4. For the filling, heat the oil in a wok over high heat, then add the mushrooms and ginger and stir-fry for 2–3 minutes, until softened. Add the scallions, bean sprouts, and shrimp and remove from the heat.

5. Divide the filling among the crepes. Brush the edges with beaten egg, roll over one side to hold in the filling, then fold in the sides and roll up firmly.

6. Place enough oil for deep-frying in a saucepan or wok and heat to 350°F/180°C, or until a cube of bread browns in 30 seconds. Add the rolls in batches and deep-fry for 3–4 minutes, turning once, until golden brown.

7. Drain the rolls on paper towels and serve immediately, with soy sauce for dipping.

Serves 4

- 1¼ cups all-purpose white flour
- pinch of salt
- 1 cup lowfat milk
- 4 tbsp water
- 1 extra-large egg
- 2 tbsp peanut oil, plus extra for greasing and deep-frying

Filling
- 1 tbsp sesame oil
- 3 cups sliced oyster mushrooms
- 1 tbsp grated fresh ginger
- 6 scallions, finely sliced
- generous 2 cups bean sprouts
- 7 oz/200 g cooked, peeled shrimp
- 1 egg, beaten
- soy sauce, for dipping

Blue Cheese Waffles

1. Sift the flour, baking powder, and salt into a bowl. Add the milk, egg, and oil and beat to a smooth batter. Stir in the blue cheese and let stand for 5 minutes.

2. Lightly grease a waffle maker and heat until hot. Pour the batter into the waffle maker and cook until golden brown. Repeat, using the remaining batter, while keeping the cooked waffles warm.

3. Top each waffle with the flaked salmon and a spoonful of horseradish sauce. Season with pepper and serve with the lemon wedges.

Serves 8

* 1¼ cups all-purpose white flour
* 1½ tsp baking powder
* pinch of salt
* 1 cup milk
* 1 extra-large egg
* 2 tbsp sunflower oil, plus extra for greasing
¾ cup crumbled blue cheese

To serve
8 oz/225 g hot smoked salmon, flaked
4 tbsp horseradish sauce
pepper
lemon wedges

Asparagus Wraps

1. Sift the flour and salt into a bowl. Add the milk, water, egg, and butter and beat to a smooth, bubbly batter. Let stand for 15 minutes.

2. For the lemon butter, place the butter and lemon rind and juice in a small saucepan over low heat and heat until the butter is melted. Season to taste with pepper and keep warm.

3. Lightly brush an 8-inch/20-cm skillet and heat over medium heat. Pour in enough batter to just cover the skillet, swirling to cover in a fairly thin, even layer. Cook until the underside is golden, then flip or turn with a spatula or palette knife and cook the other side until golden brown.

4. Repeat this process, using the remaining batter. Interleave the cooked crepes with paper towels and keep warm.

5. For the filling, bring a saucepan of lightly salted water to a boil, add the asparagus, and cook for 5–6 minutes, or until just tender. Drain. Place an asparagus spear on each crepe, season to taste with salt and pepper, and roll up.

6. Cut each roll in half across the middle and serve immediately, with the lemon butter for dipping.

Serves 4

* 1¼ cups all-purpose white flour
* pinch of salt
* 1 cup milk
  scant ½ cup water
* 1 extra-large egg
* 2 tbsp melted butter
  sunflower oil, for greasing

Lemon butter
⅔ cup lightly salted butter
finely grated rind and juice of
   1 lemon

Filling
8 thick asparagus spears
salt and pepper

Jambalaya Waffles

1. Sift the flour, baking powder, salt, and allspice into a bowl. Add the tomato juice, egg, and oil and beat to a smooth batter. Stir in the rice and let stand for 5 minutes.

2. Lightly grease a waffle maker and heat until hot. Pour the batter into the waffle maker and cook until golden brown. Repeat, using the remaining batter, while keeping the cooked waffles warm.

3. For the topping, heat the oil in a wok over high heat, add the onion, green bell pepper, and celery, and stir-fry for 2 minutes. Add the thyme and chicken and stir-fry for 3–4 minutes, until cooked.

4. Add the shrimp, chorizo, and salt and pepper to taste and stir until thoroughly heated. Spoon onto the waffles and serve immediately, seasoned with extra pepper.

Serves 4

- 1¼ cups all-purpose white flour
- 1½ tsp baking powder
- pinch of salt
- ½ tsp ground allspice
- 1 cup tomato juice
- 1 extra-large egg
- 2 tbsp corn oil, plus extra for greasing
- scant 1 cup cooked long-grain rice

Topping
- 2 tbsp corn oil
- 1 onion, sliced
- 1 green bell pepper, seeded and sliced
- 1 stalk celery, sliced
- 1 tsp dried thyme
- 1 chicken breast, cut into thin strips
- 4 oz/115 g cooked, peeled shrimp
- 3 oz/85 g chorizo, thinly sliced
- salt and pepper

Index